I Left My Heart in Chinkapook
... and My Knickers in New York

Other books by this author

Humour
Crooks, Chooks and Bloody Ratbags
Another Bloody Ratbag Book
My Ratbag Relations
Hang on to Your Horses Doovers
Born to Whinge
Worser Homes and Gardens
Life on a G-String

Comment Humour
Girls Own Guide to Ego Maintenance
Australia Unbuttoned

Adolescent
Streetwise School Smart
Here's Looking at You Kid
How to Save the World Before Breakfast

I Left My Heart in Chinkapook ... and My Knickers in New York

KERRY CUE

Lothian
BOOKS

To the crew dedicated to keeping me humble – Donald, Julian and Georgina.
And to the friends who have made these trips possible.

Thomas C. Lothian Pty Ltd
11 Munro Street, Port Melbourne, Victoria 3207

Copyright text and illustrations © Kerry Cue 1998
First published 1998

All rights reserved. No part of this publication may be reproduced, stored in a retrieval system or transmitted in any form by any means without the prior permission of the copyright owner. Enquiries should be made to the publisher.

National Library of Australia
Cataloguing-in-Publication data:
   Cue, Kerry, 1952-
   I left my heart in Chinkapook and my knickers in New York
   ISBN 0 85091 934 7

   1. Australian wit and humour. 2. Travellers' writings, Australian.
   3. Europe - Description and travel - Humour. I. Title.
   914.14

Cover design by Modern Art Production Group
Cover illustration by Tracie Grimwood
Text illustrations by Kerry Cue with some help from Georgina Cue
Design by Paulene Meyer
Printed in Australia by Griffin Press Pty Limited,
A division of PMP Communications

CONTENTS

FREE AT LAST! FREE AT LAST! For Two Weeks, Three at a Push   7

1 ADVENTURES IN THE LAND OF OZ   10
- On the Road to Gundagai and Other Places   10
- The Farm   11
- The Classic Caravan Holiday   20
- The *Princess of Tasmania*   25
- The Country Town   33
- The Centre by Bus   36
- The Bushwalk   42
- Sailing the Whitsundays   47
- Surfers with the Kids   52

2 THIS TRAVELLING LIFE or How to Organise the Mid-life Crisis For Fun and Profit   55
- Anywhere is Good at This Time of the Year!   55
- Zen and The Art of Drinking Chianti on a Terrace in Tuscany   57
- Geography and Why I Should Have Paid More Attention in Class   58
- Ms Werewolf in London   60
- How to Avoid Being Mistaken for a Columbian Drug Lord and Other Handy Travel Hints   64

3 IS THIS AIR PSYCHOTIC or Do All Pilots Think 'We're Goin' Down Jokes' Are Funny?   82
- Getting There, Sort Of   82
- The Lowdown on Flying High   84
- I'm Heaving on a Jet Plane   86
- Catch 22 Revisited or Everything You'd Like to Know About Air Travel But Have Been too Drunk to Ask   88
- The Rent-A-Car Was Fine, I'm Returning My Husband!   93

4 EUROPE: The Pink, Green and Yellow Bits   **98**
   The Netherlands: Clogs, Sex and Bicycles   99
   France: Long Live *Joie de Vivre*!   104
   There Will Always Be an England and a VAT   114
   Ireland To Be Sure, To Be Sure   121
   This is Wales, Boy-O!   130
   Scotland: Land of Lochs and Rocks   132
   Italy or How Hard Can Life Be in a Villa in Tuscany?   138
   We're Goin' Home   143
   European Epilogue or Please Remind Me Why We Did This Again!   145

5 JAPAN: The Land Where They Can't Say 'No'   **148**
   The Bonsai Bra   149
   The Land of the Vibrating Chair   151
   In Japan, Girls Just Want to Have Fun   154

6 DESPERATELY SEEKING AMERICA   **157**
   You Say 'Have a Nice Day'; We Say 'Bugger Off'   157
   Don't Shoot! I'm a Tourist   161
   The Stars at Night Have No Cellulite Deep in the Heart of LA   164
   Who Ya Gonna Call?   167
   This is the Dawning of the Middle Age of Aquarius   168
   Escape to Alcatraz   170
   If I Can Make it (Across the Road) There, I Can Make it Anywhere — New York, New York   171
   Liberty! She's My Kinda Gal!   174
   Washington: Centre of the Free World   175
   Vote [1] Barbie For President   182
   Damned Lies and Statistics or More About Sex and Americans   184
   Lost in the Knickers of Time   186
   Missing You Already, America   189

EPILOGUE   **191**

FREE AT LAST! FREE AT LAST!
For Two Weeks, Three at a Push

Something uncanny takes place in the landscape of your mind when you travel. Your senses and perceptions are jarred into a new reality. At home, the edges of your brain can be worn flat by the dreary familiarity of everyday life. That spark of curiosity, the flame of fascination, don't even flicker in your own home town.

We are most often the worst tourists at home. Familiarity blinds us to the potential of our surroundings. We couldn't pay less attention than we do to the historical landmarks and statues dotted about our own town, suburb or street. The neighbourhood pigeons pay more attention to the local statues than we do.

Yet, we travel thousands of miles to stand and have our picture taken with a statue of some civic personage from somewhere else, with great enthusiasm and interest, while our own images of history rarely penetrate our conscious thoughts.

So travel is, above all else, a great stimulant for the brain. A mind tonic. A soul revitaliser. For in the shadows of every photograph can be found a philosophical thought questioning so many facets of existence, or, more specifically, the many facets of how we choose to exist.

Travel also provides freedom. As soon as we step out of childhood, life loads us up with responsibilities. And the further we journey through life, the bigger, it seems, is the load. But travel offers a respite from serious life citizenship. Forget the studies. Forget the career. (Work travel offers no such respite from reality, for, if nothing else, you are lugging along your career with you, and all its weighty angsts and frustrations.) Forget family duty — except perhaps for a postcard, which in my case I usually manage to post just as I'm boarding the plane for the home trip.

Forget the mortgage, paying the bills, weeding the garden, booking the car in for its overdue service, feeding the cat, trying to think what you are going to cook for dinner tonight and how much fibre you have in your diet, and go. Just go. Free at last! Free at last! If only for three weeks.

Travel also provides soul food for the traveller in the form of hope. The image we have of the world, created so often by the media, is a broad canvas painted over and over in sombre tones of despair and destruction. The world, we begin to believe, is dying.

But to travel is to stumble across scene after scene of such rugged splendour and timeless magnificence that your emotions overwhelm your senses. You feel a lump in your throat. You may even weep. Joyful tears. For if this place exists, then there is hope yet for our world.

To travel is to know irony. Wherever you travel in the world someone else's ordinariness becomes your Grand Opera.

To travel is also to explore many of the shadows of your own psyche, for different people find beauty in different things. I know of one couple who cannot travel together. She, for instance, cannot see anything moving about the Grand Canyon: 'It's just a hole in the ground,' she mumbles. While he cannot see beauty in the works of the Great Masters: 'Why would you travel that far to look at the Mona Lisa? You can buy her here on a key ring, and take her with you at a fraction of the cost!' Soul food comes in different packages.

To travel is to experience some of the mysterious murmurings of the underworld. You may find yourself walking for the first time down a small cobbled back lane in Paris ... you feel your hair prickle at the back of your neck as you realise, 'I've been here before. I know this place.' What corner of your soul knows this? Or what ghost has come calling to remind you of your place in the grand scheme of the human saga? Then you may turn the corner to have familiarity thrust in your face. 'Ah, yes! McDonald's.'

The magic of travel is everywhere in the world. The tragedy, the drama, the pathos of past human struggle haunts every grand ruin, and you feel the tormented or triumphant ghosts echoing in your every step.

Travel renews your childish sense of wonder because the world, indeed, has many wonders. Sometimes wonder can be found on a small scale. In one waterlily, you may see Monet's garden, for a single lily can reflect so much beauty seen so differently through an old painter's eyes.

Other times, the wonder is seen on a spectacular scale. To view the unbelievable drama of the almost peak-perfect Italian Alps, or to stand and absorb the hauntingly prehistoric forms of our Grampian mountains, is to feel for a moment like a mere speck of existence in the infinite continuum of the universe — a humbling experience.

And to travel is to know irony. For wherever you go in the world there is someone mopping the floor of the Louvre in Paris, yawning as they take your car parking fee in Florence, or snoozing while they stand packed like a sardine into a peak hour train in Tokyo.

In other words, wherever you travel in the world someone else's ordinariness becomes your Grand Opera.

ONE
ADVENTURES IN THE LAND OF OZ

ON THE ROAD TO GUNDAGAI AND OTHER PLACES

When I began to sift through my memories of travelling I discovered, first and foremost, they tell a story of a lifetime of travel. My parents believed that children were best educated by taking them places. And so they packed however many children there were at the time — we peaked at five — into the little green Vauxhall, or the FC Holden with the reconditioned engine, or later, the FE with the stiff column gear shift. We would hook on the caravan, at first a heavy plywood affair shaped like a flat-sided egg, and later, many cramped holidays later, our own second-hand Viscount caravan and head off to:

- *the Mallee* — 'that's where Grandma and Pop had their farm,' says Dad. 'We were burnt out during the Depression.'
  'Why were you depressed, Dad?'
  'Are you being funny?'
- *the Kiewa Valley Hydro-electric Scheme* — 'but how do they make electricity out of water, Dad?'
  'They ... um ... see those machines ... they um ... just shut up and listen to the guide.'
- *the Sydney Harbour Bridge* — 'it was built like a Meccano Set.'
  'Can I have one for Christmas?'
  'And what are you goin' to do with a Sydney Harbour Bridge? Eh?'

- *Parkes, ACT* — 'I was stationed here during the War.'
  'Was the War in Parkes, Dad?'
  'No.'

- *The Gap, Sydney* — 'people jump off here and drown themselves.'
  'Why?'
  'People in Sydney are a bit odd.'
  'Aw.'

- *Canberra War Museum* — 'but you were in the War, Dad, they haven't got your name on the list.'
  'For goodness sake. They only put up the names of those who were killed.'
  'Oh.'

It is only now as I flick back through my holiday memory banks that I realise so many of the holidays I had constituted the typical Aussie experience of the time. These holidays were executed with my family's own particular brand of drama and chaos. They were determined by available cash — not much — and circumstance — 'We'll go in the September school holidays. Two weeks will be enough.' Our holidays were always genuine comedies of their era.

And so the trips I have enjoyed — sometimes endured — from the great caravan epic, to crossing Bass Strait on the *Princess of Tasmania*, to sailing the Whitsundays, to doing the great bushwalk, to travelling to the centre by bus, to doing Surfers, have all been, in their own way, Aussie classics.

THE FARM

It's the 1950s, and every Australian has relatives on the land. Cousins, grandparents, or some relation, somewhere. My father has more cousins than most. They are spread throughout the Mallee from Manangatang to Quambatook, from Patchewollock to Wycheproof, or thereabouts.

He was born in the bush in 1922, near Nyah West. We have a photograph of him as a baby with Old Shep, the sheep dog, but the fires came and burnt them out. It was the Depression and the bank foreclosed. So my father, the eldest child, his brother and two sisters were bundled on to a train and shunted off to Melbourne and a new life.

My Aunty Dot can remember the four of them being left on St Kilda beach while their parents went off to look for lodgings. And the children, terrified that they might lose their boots, buried them in the sand and waited.

That boy, my father, waiting on a beach in a bustling suburb of Melbourne, longed, always longed, to return to the bush. To that gravelly, spindly, scrubby part of north-western Victoria where farmers push the boundaries of hope further and further into the Mallee scrub to be beaten back, time and again, by drought, fire, salinity levels, and by the vagaries of world economics. It is always a battle for existence fought on a thin skin of topsoil.

Because my father's heart always lay in this rugged, untameable part of Australia, whenever I visit the Mallee I leave my heart there, too, in Nyah West, Chinkapook, Quambatook, Kerang, Manangatang. And I think of my father, for he never returned to the Mallee. War intervened first, then a career in the police force.

But at least I understand now why he persevered — and perseverance only describes in small part the enormity of the effort required to get my family on the road — in taking us as children to visit this cousin's farm or that cousin's farm in his heartland, the Mallee scrub.

'Where are we goin' again?'

'We're going to Uncle Keith's farm,' explains Father securing the pack-rack on our old Vauxhall.

'Who is Uncle Keith? I didn't know we had an Uncle Keith,' I mumble wiping my nose on my cardigan sleeve.

'Don't do that,' insists Father. 'Haven't you got a hankie?'

'Nup,' I sniff.

'Don't sniff.'

'What am I meant to do then?'

'Go and see your mother.'

'I'm okay. But who is this Uncle Keith?'

'He's not an uncle,' sighs Father. 'He's a cousin of mine. But uncle will do. Now get in the car.'

'Stop that,' yells my father at my elder brother. Brian is dragging the dog along the front lawn by its teeth, which happen to be firmly embedded in the sleeve of his jumper.

'That's your school jumper,' huffs Father.
'Can we take Jippy with us?' pleads Brian.
'No. He's a city dog. He'll just go silly and chase sheep.'
'But he'd love it on the farm,' enthuses Brian.
'You're lucky I'm taking *you*. Let alone the dog. Now lock him in the backyard and get in the car.'

Our mother finally emerges from the back door with the baby on her hip, a bag full of nappies, a plastic shopping bag full of sandwiches and the three-year-old dressed as a cowboy. She has that certain look on her face that sends our father galloping to slam the back door so our mother cannot escape back into the house after some forgotten thing.

'Come on Hop-Along-Cassidy. Get in the car. It's a long drive to the country,' urges Father.

'Will there be Indians?'

'Of course there aren't any Indians. Ya dumdum,' scoffs his elder brother. 'This is Australia.'

'But I wanna shoot Indians,' sniffs the pint-sized cowboy.

'Ya can shoot whatever ya like. Just get in the car.'

The canvas baby seat is hooked over the back of the bench-seat. The baby is dropped in. We're loaded and ready.

Father turns the ignition key. Cough. Splutter. Cough. Nothing. Nothing.

'Jesus bloody wept,' he snaps through gritted teeth.

'Now don't any of you get out of the car.'

He digs around the boot of the car then returns to the front. He puts the crank handle under the grill. Winds once. Nothing. Winds twice. Nothing. Winds again. Splutter. Splutter. K-chug. K-chug. K-chug. We're in business. Off we go.

Somewhere in the bush

'Where are we going?' I ask as my father puts his hand out the window to signal a right-hand turn.

'Do you have to ask right at this minute?' complains Father. 'Look at that. Did you see that Kath? That fool of a driver's meant to give way to me. I have a good mind to book him.' My father could never forget he was a policeman.

'Not now Jack,' consoles Mother. 'We'll never get there.'

'Hmmph,' snorts Father.

'Are we nearly there yet?' whinges the three-year-old.

'For goodness sake. We haven't even left the city yet,' replies Father.

'Where's there?' I moan. 'Where are we goin'?'

'I told you. We're going to the Mallee where I grew up. Near where Grandma and Pop had the farm at Tittybong.'

'Tittybong!' I snigger.

'Titty-bong-titty-bong ... titty-bong-bong-bong,' chortles Brian the eldest.

'Honestly,' grumbles my father. 'I don't know why I bother sometimes.'

'Tell us, Dad. Tell us about when you were a kid.'

'I had to milk half a dozen cows then deliver the milk on horseback for a ha'penny, I think it was, before school.'

'You had a horse. You were lucky. Why can't we have a horse?' I grizzle.

'I wanna horse,' adds the horseless cowboy.

'Oh for God's sake,' moans Father. 'Don't any of you ever shut up?'

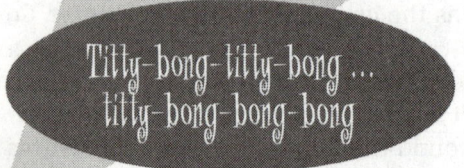

By lunchtime the car has over-heated. Father opens the radiator cap with a rag. Steam pours out.

We stop by the side of the road to eat our Stras and pickle sandwiches under the thin shade of a gum tree, shooing off the pesky bush flies. Father goes off seeking water from a farm dam.

'Don't any of you go wandering off,' he calls over his shoulder.

But we do. We find anthills to poke sticks into, rabbit burrows to look down and feathers to collect.

Eventually, in a hysteria of urgency, Father orders us back into the car. We're on our way again. By mid afternoon with our sweaty thighs sticking to the hard surface of the car seat, we are niggly, uncomfortable and bored. We start pushing each other in the back.

'Brian put his foot on me.'

'Well don't,' snaps Father.

'Kerry's leaning on me. Get her off.'

In the end Father drives with one hand on the steering wheel and leans over the back of his seat to whack kids at random. It is his policy to hit first and ask questions later.

One kid always complains. 'It's not fair. I didn't do nothin'.'

Father's standard reply is: 'Stop ya whingin'. It'll even out on a long trip.'

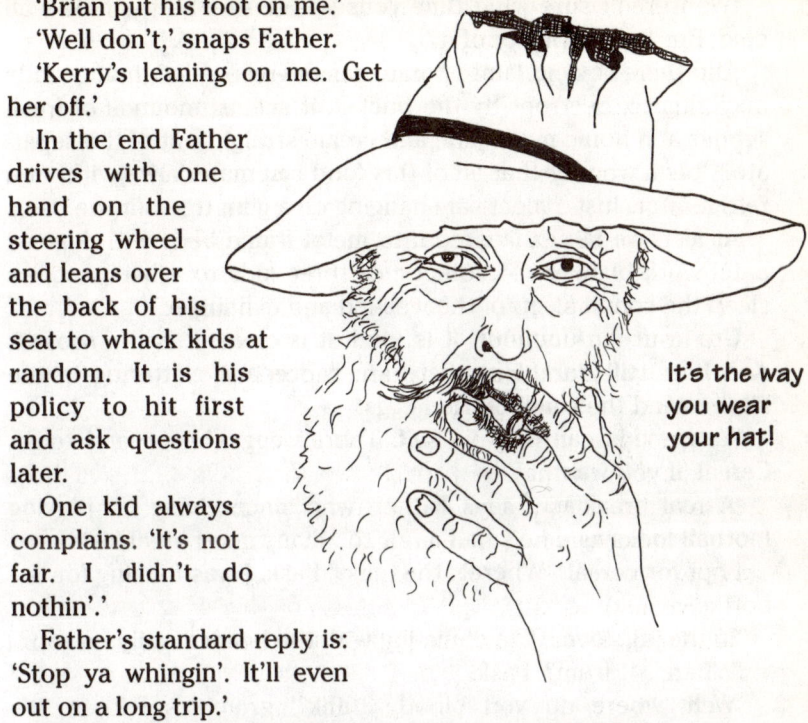

It's the way you wear your hat!

Finally we arrive at the farm on dusk — a carload of discontent. The farm dogs bark and dance at the end of their chains heralding our arrival. And it is a brave new world for us.

The aunty and uncle that we didn't know we had come out of the house. He's in boots 'n' braces and checked shirt, wearing a beaten army hat even though it's dark. She's plump and in a floral dress, wiping her hands dry on her apron. And there are kids hanging about behind their parents, giving the city kids the up and down eyeball and the good once-over.

We walk into the kitchen and back in time by three decades. There is no power. Just the hissing of the hurricane lamp in the middle of the table and the sharp shadows prancing around the bare walls. A few strips of flypaper dotted with flies hang in the doorway. The sink is a deep ceramic trough with a lone brass tap and a curtained-off section for the saucepans beneath. The cooking range uses wood. There are a few Mallee roots, twisted and gnarled, resting on the hearth. And the kettle, heavy cast iron and black, is on the stove, boiling.

'We weren't sure what time youse'd get 'ere. So the food's all cold. But there's plenty of it.'

And there is: cold lamb; potato salad; green salad; home-made mayonnaise; beetroot by the bucket, it seems; mounds of fresh scones and home-made jam; and cream straight out of the separator. It is a wonder that all of this food can materialise without a refrigerator. Just a meat safe hanging on a gum tree out the back.

At last, we fall exhausted into metal frame beds with knitted patchwork blankets — sometimes three kids to a bed. And we sleep the sound sleep of the well-fed and exhausted.

Urp-ur-urp-ur-uuuuuur! It is loud. It is close. It is the rooster. And it is still dark. But there are saucepans clattering in the kitchen and the smell of fried eggs.

'Youse kids can help ya self. There's eggs, bacon and toast. Cereal, if you want it.'

'A real breakfast,' says Father, who since giving up playing football looks as if he's had a few too many good breakfasts.

I opt for cereal. 'Where's the milk?' I ask. I was looking for the bottle.

'In the jug, love.' The china jug with the beaded doily on top.

'Where's it from?' I ask.

'Well, where do you bloody think?' grumbles Father. 'It's straight out of the cow.'

I smell the jug and wrinkle my nose. I try a bit in a glass. 'Eh! That's disgusting,' I protest. 'It tastes like cow.'

Father rolls his eyes in despair. We were city kids. We drank only bottled milk; so we nearly choked every morning eating our Rice Bubbles dry.

And so it went. Much to our father's frustration, our dose of being up bush only convinced us kids that the city was a great place to be.

'Oh God. It was revolting,' I cough, almost spewing. 'There were guts everywhere. And blood.' I'd been in the machine shed-cum-slaughter house.

'And where, young lady, do you think legs of lamb come from? Do you reckon they grow on bloody trees?'

'Turn that tap off. It's tank water. Don't waste a drop,' protests Father.

'It tastes like something died in it,' I hiss.

'Oh yeah. We had a cockatoo drown in the tank one year.'

'Errr!' There was a collective groan from the city kids.

But worst of all was the dunny. The stinky tin-shed of a dunny. The long drop out the back with wind whistling through the nail holes, spider webs all around, a wooden bench-seat with the heaviest lid ever invented, and squares of newspaper for the user's convenience.

'Newspaper,' I whisper to my mother. 'They've got newspaper in the dunny.'

'Oh yeah,' sings the woman of the house. 'That newsprint is pretty rough on ya backside. Ya end up with the black hole of Calcutta. That's what his nibs calls it.'

But Father was in his element helping out on the farm. Cutting chaff, he'd throw a stray mouse our way and send kids scrambling in every direction. Milking a cow by hand, he'd squirt us with milk. Knackering lambs, he'd joke that he was 'doin' it with his teeth'. But I knew he was joking. He had false teeth. I figured he'd lose his teeth before a lamb lost any of its vital bits.

All the time Father was trying to show us how wonderful life was on the land and all the time, despite revelling in rides on the tractor and falling over one another riding round the bush block in the back of the ute, we children entertained grave doubts.

The farm I remember most clearly was Aunty Ivy's. Aunty Ivy was not our aunty. She was my cousins' grandma, sort of. But everyone called her Aunty Ivy. She had a farm spread out over luxurious acres at Red Cliffs, which was also in the Mallee.

The farm stretched on forever to a flat, flat horizon. All around were rocks, stones and red dust puffing around each footprint and billowing behind each car that came roaring into the home paddock.

The gum trees that grew there were thin, scrappy and struggled to keep a root-hold in the gravelly earth. There were, in fact, so few trees around the farmhouse that when the dogs dug out a goanna and chased it, the miniature dragon-like reptile ran for refuge up my Uncle Mick. He was my real uncle — my mother's brother, and Aunty Ivy's son-in-law, sort of. He was tall, my Uncle Mick, a good 1.8 metres (6 feet 2 inches). And the goanna sat terrified on his head and dug in its claws.

Uncle Mick was not very happy with this turn of events because every time he knocked the goanna off his head, it ran back up his leg again. He had to give it a good swift kick in the guts to get it to rethink its position in life and find another tree.

I gathered from the whispering and nodding of the adults, that Aunty Ivy had money. She employed a manager to run the mostly wheat and sheep property. And Aunty Ivy did unheard of things like buy a new car when it *was* new. I was intrigued by the adult whisperings. I expected on my arrival at Aunty Ivy's farm to see money sticking out of drawers in the farmhouse. But I never did see any so she couldn't have been that rich.

The farmhouse was low and flat with a few vines growing on a trellis at the back door — the only attempt at a garden. Otherwise the farm settlement was all corrugated iron sheds, windmills and water tanks.

One night we went on a kangaroo hunt. The kangaroos had been travelling through the farm in packs trampling the wheat crop. Something had to be done. Besides, the dogs needed some meat. I was eight years old and allowed to sit in the cabin of one ute as long as I piped down and didn't get in the way.

The men stood with their guns on the tray of each ute and held on to the open window of the cabin. The driver of my ute worked the steering wheel with one hand and held the spotlight with the other.

I sat silent and spellbound throughout the hunt. For nothing compares with a kangaroo hunt. Later, when our family moved to a country police station not far from Melbourne, I used to go rabbiting and fox hunting. There was a bounty on fox scalps at the time, and rabbits fetched 7s 6d a pair, if they were shot clean through the head. I was often out in a ute working the spotlight; usually the rabbits just sat there. Bang. No chance. The foxes were cunning though and hard to catch in the spot. But hunting kangaroos. This was a challenge. It was a high speed chase, abandoning all caution, bumping up and down across the paddock on full throttle.

The day of the kangaroo hunt was hot but the night comes cold and crisp, a desert night with no moon. We are surrounded by ink blackness broken only by the headlights clinging to the spiky grass track and scenes caught for a moment in the spotlight — an arbour of trees, an owl, a creaking windmill, or the green-glowing eyes of stunned sheep.

We drive slowly down towards the bush block scanning grazing paddock after grazing paddock with the roving spotlight. There is no sign of a kangaroo. Then comes the shout, 'There they are.' I see bounding shadows several hundred metres away. The utes head straight across the open flats of cut hay paddocks after the mob, although there are stones, rabbit burrows and erosion cracks to worry about. Our ute hits 50 kph, 60, 70, and beyond.

The driver swings the steering wheel with his one hand to avoid obstacles while keeping that spotlight dead ahead on his bounding prey. The ute bounces, snakes and broadsides across the paddock. I hold on to my seat and the door. And still I bounce.

There is a shout. The ute stops one hundred metres from the corner of the paddock next to the gate. A mother throws her joe out of her pouch and bounds on. The shooters are ready. Bang. And again. And again. But the kangaroos are over the fence and gone in an instant into the bush paddock.

'Damn, hell, and blast,' snorts my father. 'This rifle bolt is jammed.'

All that remains in the spotlight is the joey. The little thing was stunned; sleeping one minute, thrown out of home the next.

'We'd better pick it up,' says Uncle Mick. 'It hasn't got a hope out here.' Off goes Uncle Mick, all 1.8 metres of him to catch the tiny joey. It hops out of his reach over and over.

We're all laughing. Finally he throws his coat over it. 'They're a cow of a thing to look after, joeys. Fussy,' complains my uncle.

'I'll do it. I'll do it,' volunteers Ricky, my cousin. So the joey ends up in the ute at my feet.

'They're in the bush paddock. Come on.' We head through the gate. This time in a paddock of low scrub and spindly eucalypts we have to stick to the bulldozed track along the fence line. We move down the tunnel of light. Suddenly the mob jumps out ahead of us. We're off chasing the 'roos. Faster. Faster. They don't go back into the bush. They bound ahead of us — eight 'roos maybe. We get close. A kangaroo in full bound is a vision of rhythm, harmony and balance.

'Ready,' shouts my driver. The utes kick up dust as they stop. Bang. And again. And again. But only one 'roo hits the dust. My father gets out to look at the kill. It's an old red male. He's big. He gets up. Rears up on his hind legs. He looks three metres tall. Big black claws. I think he's going to kill my father. I see Dad in the headlights, steady his gun, aim, bang. The buck drops. The men drag the carcass to the back of the ute. Its body is warm and floppy and it is hard to load on to the tray. That was the only kill for the night.

'Might keep 'em away for a while,' says the manager.

It's back to the farmhouse. The dogs go wild because they can smell the blood. And there is a joey to look after.

I'm floating somewhere outside of my head, pumped up with adrenalin, thinking that life in the bush is too many things rushing at you at once.

Life. Death. Survival. The hunt.

THE CLASSIC CARAVAN HOLIDAY

It was my father's dream, this caravan. A marvel of the modern era of transportation. But this was the 1960s, and the marvel was a Viscount caravan. Bought secondhand, it was aluminium clad, but heavy and ponderous and an unfair burden on its little wheels.

My father could never get that tyre pressure right. When the air pressure was low, the caravan was so sluggish, we feared we would have to get out and push the old FC Holden with the reconditioned engine up every hill. When the tyres were rock hard, the caravan almost bounced along the Princes Highway. We'd stop for lunch to find the next day's breakfast had exploded in a shower of Rice Bubbles inside the van.

Father loved that van. 'Not bad. Eh! Five berth,' he'd say, affectionately patting the side of the van. It didn't seem to bother him that there were actually seven of us. 'The boys can sleep in the annexe,' says Father. 'We don't have an annexe,' replies mother. 'We'll get one.' But there wasn't much spare cash between pay packets for a policeman with five kids, and annexes cost a few quid. So Dad got this idea. 'Kath you can sew,' he says. 'Not a caravan ANNEXE!' she protests. But she does. Father borrows an old treadle sewing machine and Mum sews canvas for a week. Father helps. Every so often he digs Mother and the sewing machine out of several folding layers of canvas.

Father loved that van. But, by God, he could have done with a holiday without us. Our first caravan trip was to Lakes Entrance,

Victoria. As usual, leaving was murder. 'Right. We're going,' he'd say. Doors opened, doors closed, as kids jumped in and out of the car. In the end Father would just drive off. This was mostly successful though one time we left the baby in a pusher in a car park. And it was only with a certain reluctance that Father returned to pick her up.

Once on the road, Father wouldn't stop. One of us kids, sitting with clammy legs clinging to the hot vinyl bench-seat in the back would complain, 'I wanna go to the toilet.' 'In a minute,' Father would reply. That minute stretched on to eternity. When, thirty kilometres later, Father stopped the car, you'd shoot into the public toilet block like a rocket and pee like a typhoon and Father would still be pacing outside the car mumbling, 'You took your bloody time.'

The first night in Traralgon Mum lit the kero stove. And whoosh! There is a flash of flame; the stove's on fire, curtains too. Dad is fiddling under the bonnet of the car. I race out and yell, 'The caravan's on fire.' Dad bangs his head on the bonnet. Then he rushes in and throws the stove out the door. Drama's over. And Dad says to me, 'You could give a man a bloody heart attack doing that.' Fish 'n' chips that night but they tasted of kero.

At bedtime I get a bunk in the van. The baby's in a drawer — open, of course — the three boys are in the annexe. The worry is Geoff who is a sleepwalker. 'I'll sort it out,' says Father. And he does. Geoff gets nicely settled in his sleeping bag then Dad ties him to the stretcher with electrical flex. It solved the problem. Years later, Geoff says, 'I felt like one of those mummies in a horror movie. I'd lie there all night and could only move my eyeballs.'

Dad gets up early and unties his son. He wake us up but his teenage son won't wake. In the end Father drops the annexe on him. Brian crawls out muttering, 'What's goin' on?' 'We're leaving,' huffs Father. Mum is away socialising at the laundry block. Teenage son is given the job of filling the water tank. Simple enough. He falls asleep on the job and fills the caravan to the depth of ten centimetres wetting all our bedding in the process. Mum opens the caravan door to the Great Flood.

'We're leaving,' says Father. 'What about the bedding? I've got to dry it,' says Mother. 'We can hang it out the windows of the car as we drive along,' says Father. We do.

In the meantime everyone is eating tomatoes. 'I don't like tomatoes,' not at ten in the morning. But there's a fruit fly inspection coming up. 'Eat,' says Father. And we eat. Tomatoes and oranges.

So passes the first twenty-four hours of our caravan holiday. We had two weeks altogether. I don't know how Father with his iffy blood pressure survived. He did though. He survived just long enough to go back to work. But we loved the whole catastrophe.

Later, much later, my father took long service leave from the police force.

'We'll take the caravan,' he says. 'And visit Mick and Noela at Caloundra.' Uncle Mick has moved from the dust-red Mallee to a beachfront property with swaying palms in tropical Queensland.

But there is a bit of a juggle with the kids. Brian, the eldest, is doing an apprenticeship.

'He'll have to stay at home,' says Father. 'But that's good. He can feed the dog and the prisoners.' Mum normally fed the prisoners by throwing on a few extra potatoes whenever Father rang through to the police residence saying, 'We've got another one.' Not that there were many prisoners. Maybe one inmate for a weekend before he was whisked off in a police car to a city remand centre.

So it was decided with great enthusiasm all around that Brian would feed the prisoners. This, of course, was without asking Brian.

'I'm not gonna feed prisoners!'

'It's not hard,' explains Father. 'The constable on duty will open the cell door and you put the tray down. It's as simple as that.'

'You've gotta cook for yourself anyway,' reminds Mother. 'Add a bit more if there's a prisoner. That's all you have to do.'

'I'm not gonna cook,' gasps the shocked youth.

'What are you going to do?' asks his mother.

'Eat fish 'n' chips.'

'For six weeks?'

'You've got to open a can to feed the dog. The very least you can do is open a can or two for the prisoners,' insists his father.

So amid mutterings of dissent Brian became the short-order cook. And no penal institution could inflict a more devious punishment than the menu devised by the Police Sergeant's son at the Kyneton watchhouse.

There were some prisoners while we were away. One detainee scored three days in the local lockup.

'What'd ya feed 'im?' asks Father later.

'Baked beans on toast,' replies Brian.

'What about for lunch?'

'Baked beans on toast.'

'Dinner?'

You guessed. 'Baked beans on toast.' Every meal.

'All baked beans?' asks Father.

'Yep.'

'Why?'

'Those tins were the closest,' replies the youth.

'Poor blighter,' sniffs my father.

The other major decision of the trip was that I, the university student, would drive my car, the Morris Minor, in convoy with the family car and caravan. This was a cunning plan of Father's. There were my two younger brothers, aged ten and twelve, and the new addition, my baby sister, to think about. Travelling in two cars meant he could split my brothers and save himself the agony of sorting out arguments for 1200 painfully long kilometres. Off we set.

I can confidently say if you drive up the Newell Highway in a Morris Minor you gain a new understanding of the word flat. That stretch from Gilgandra to Goondiwindi is wondrous in that overwhelming I'm-in-the-middle-of-nowhere sort of way, but it is flat, featureless and repetitive. There isn't even a bend in the road to add some sort of exciting highlight to the trip.

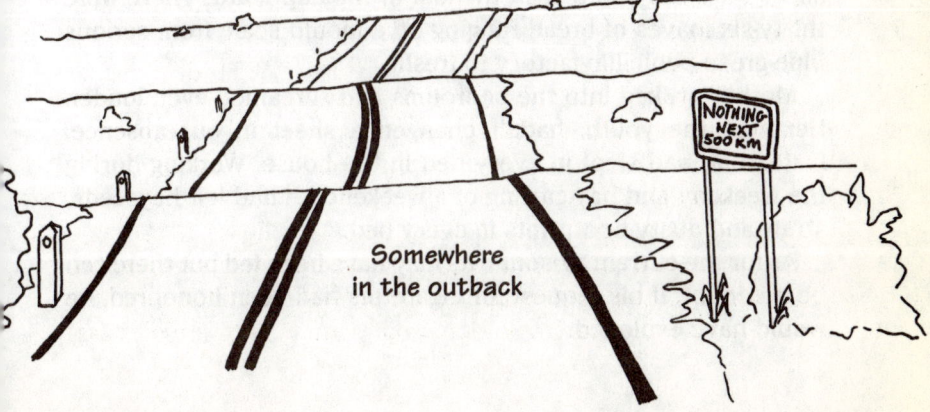

Somewhere in the outback

Somewhere around Moree I had a great idea to relieve the boredom. 'Let's play a trick on Dad,' I enthuse, addressing the passenger of the day, namely, my twelve-year-old brother Geoffrey.

'Yeah. Let's. What?'

'I'll drop you off at the side of the road and when Dad comes along with the caravan, you pretend you're hitch-hiking.'

'Yeah,' says young and gullible.

So I stop the car and leave a twelve-year-old in the middle of flat bloody nowhere. And I don't look back.

Anyway, our father drives up an hour later towing the van. He stops. My brother runs up and jumps in the car. His father leans over the front seat and goes 'Whop'. He gives Geoff a decent biff on the ears.

'Jesus,' shouts Father. 'See! Even ya sister can't stand ya.'

'Great joke,' sneers Geoff later.

It took us five days to reach Caloundra. But after that the holiday was nothing but a blur of languid days at the beach, barbecues at dusk, film nights on deckchairs and, for the boys, cane toad hunting at night by torchlight.

Six weeks later the Meehan family touring cavalcade returns home.

Our mother walks into the house and screams. Her son, the youth in charge of the house, hasn't washed a dish in six weeks. There are five shades of mould growing on plates stacked in and around the sink.

She opens a cupboard and screams again. She had forgotten to cancel the bread. The thought hadn't struck her son, the youth, that he didn't need a loaf of bread every day. He just took out two slices for toast and tossed the loaf in the cupboard. There were thirty-six loaves of bread ranging on a mould scale from serious blue-green penicillin-factory to fresh.

Mother walked into the bedrooms and screamed even louder. Her son, the youth, hadn't changed a sheet in our absence. Instead he had slept in every bed in the house. Working during the weekday and hay-carting of a weekend he had left hayseeds, straw and dusty bootprints in every bed.

As for the current prisoner, he may have been fed but there can be no doubt, if his request for cigarettes had been honoured, he would have exploded.

THE PRINCESS OF TASMANIA

It was the early 1970s when love, peace and flower children were ostensibly poised to bring about a new world order. And I was poised to bring about a new family order. I was heading off on a major trip, this time, by myself. When I say 'by myself' I mean, I was heading for high adventure with a university friend, a borrowed backpack, a Youth Hostel guidebook and a burst of youthful enthusiasm emanating from me in a naive glow.

'I am a woman of the world now Dad,' I insist with the full momentum of nineteen-year-old confidence. 'I'm hitch-hiking around Tasmania. And that's that.'

'You are bloody not,' grumps my father shovelling a dessert-spoon full of sugar on to his Corn Flakes.

'That stuff's no good for you,' I protest haughtily.' All that sugar'll rot ya insides.'

'Hmmph,' he grumps.

'Now Jack. She's not a child,' coos Mother. My mother wasn't the sort to coo often. She was more the guffawing type, always finding something ridiculous — usually one of us — to laugh about. But, when the dove-like sounds of peaceful cooing were required. She could coo.

'She's at university,' continues Mother.

'Uni-bloody-versity,' barks my father. 'Long-haired layabouts the lot of 'em. They've got all the time in the world to march up and down Bourke Street to protest about the Vietnam war. But no time to get a decent bloody haircut. Or a decent job.'

'Oh that's so typical of you. Put them all in the army. Send them all over to Vietnam. Do them good.'

'Too bloody right,' he agrees, putting another spoonful of sugar on his Corn Flakes.

'How did we get to Vietnam?' coos Mother, 'I thought we were talking about Tasmania.'

'And another thing,' I blurt. 'You wouldn't let me go parachuting. Oh no. If the army's so good for everyone, why won't you let me jump out of a plane?'

'Kerry,' coos Mother.

'And I'm going on the next moratorium. And I don't care if I'm arrested. By you.'

'KERRY,' urges Mother through gritted teeth. 'There's something I want to show you.' She pulls me out the kitchen door by the back loop of my hipster jeans.

'You'd reckon he was born last century,' I complain in the hall. 'Hitch-hiking around Tasmania. It's nothing. He's an old ... old ... old whatever-he-is.'

'Just calm down and leave it to me,' sighs Mother.

I went to Tassie.

My father stood, arms folded, in the passengers' lounge (a rather generous term for what amounted to an oversized garden shed with bench-seats), casting a pall of gloom over the *bon voyage* frivolity.

'You didn't have ta come,' I sigh. 'All the way from the country for two minutes to say goodbye.'

'Hmmph,' (my father's favourite expression).

'Jack. You could be a little bit more cheerful,' cajoles Mother in her best hat as she rummages in her handbag to find a hankie to wipe my four-year-old sister's nose. 'We're not exactly visiting her on death row, you know.'

'Kewie. Where? Stop. Ya hurtin' my knowth,' protests my sister with a lisp. She'd knocked out a tooth recently with a tin whistle and our mother tended to wipe your nose by trying to pull it off your face.

'Where ya goin' to?' persists the little voice fending off Mother's second assault with a clean patch of the hankie.

'To Tasmania.'

'Dad's mania?' she mimicks.

'Yeah! It's Dad's mania, all right,' I wholeheartedly agree.

'Hmmph,' he snorts.

'Oh God, Dad,' I moan. 'I am not a child. Look. There's Jan.' Jan Swinburne, my co-conspirator in reckless adventure, has bounded in the door.

'She's a lovely girl,' chortles Mother. 'You be nice to the girl, Jack.'

'Hmmph,' replies Father.

'Hello Mr Meehan. Mrs Meehan.' Jan dumps her backpack at our feet. 'Ahh! It feels like I've got a brick in there. Mum sent some jam.'

'What do we want jam for?' I ask.

'It's not for us,' replies Jan. 'It's for your mum.'

'Oh lovely,' says Mum.

'I don't know how your father could agree to this nonsense young lady,' says Father addressing Jan in his lecturing tone. 'Him a politician and all.'

'Dad. We're not going down there to blow up parliament or anything. We're just goin' to hitch-hike for a week,' I insist.

'Bloody ridiculous,' he grumbles.

'Jack,' cautions Mother, with a don't-carry-on threat in her voice.

The ferry horn gives a long blast. After hugging my mother and sister and kissing my father — he of the wooden Indian demeanour — on his wooden cheek, we two women-of-the-world in T-shirts and shorts, wearing pigtails and chewing gum, bounce down the narrow gangplank, waving, and on to the boat.

The *Princess of Tasmania*, now retired, was a car ferry that chugged overnight from the mainland to the seventh, but occasionally forgotten, state of Tasmania below. It was a boat of very little character; the paint on the interior and exterior couldn't decide if it was dirty cream or an ageing grey. We hoped the *Princess of Tasmania* would carry us safely over the notoriously ferocious Tasman crossing. Bass Strait was world renowned. These were dangerous waters.

If all the stories were true the bed of Bass Strait should have been littered with false teeth lost by passengers heaving over the side. The ferry itself was rumoured on bad crossings to become nothing more than a slopping tub of vomit, produced by those passengers who didn't even make it to the edge. The *Princess of Tasmania* was a very ordinary boat made ominous by the power of nautical myth.

'I'm not goin' to throw up,' says Jan.

'Well, I'm not planning to either,' I reply.

'What are ya gonna have for dinner?' Jan asks. A good travelling companion, Jan never mastered the art of the diet. She didn't mind going on a diet as long as she got enough to eat. Me too. I'd go on two diets at once just to get a full plate.

We stand in the ferry cafeteria studying the menu for some time.

'I think I'll have a pie.'

'How about a pie and chips?'

'Oh look. They've got pie, chips and peas,' I enthuse. Later I would regret the peas.

'I've got it,' says Jan. 'Pie, chips, peas, trifle and sliced peaches, and a Coke.'

We sit on fixed stools at the cafeteria service bar as the *Princess of Tasmania* glides out of its Melbourne dock towards Port Phillip heads. And we are feeling unbelievably relaxed about our sea-worthiness.

The chips are real greasers — limp and soggy — and the red jelly on the trifle could have been a square chunk cut out of the lifebuoys, but we don't care. Our spirits are high, our feet well grounded and our stomachs settled comfortably somewhere in-between. We could have eaten fried eggs washed down with a warm tub of lard. No worries.

> I'd swear I can see the grim reaper walking past. She is wearing a pink linen suit.

We stow our backpacks in our allocated zone — travelling on cheap student fares, we were, alas, sitting up all night — and head off to explore the ship. We bolt up gangways and slip down others. Stride the decks. We inspect the funnels, the life rafts and the toilets. We watch the twinkling lights of Port Phillip heads fade to black on the horizon. We watch the stars. We get cold. We get bored. So we amble inside to assume our seats.

We travellers of the non-cabined classes are seated on airline-style seats in rows of twenty at the bow of the ship. With seating for, perhaps two hundred, only half the seats are filled. So we are quite comfortable. At eleven o'clock the cabin lights are dimmed and passengers begin to settle for the long haul through the night. The cabin falls into silence broken by an occasional cough or a baby's cry.

And there we sit curled in our seats trying to sleep, listening to the boat make a groaning creak as it rolls slowly to the left, then recovers to roll slowly to the right. The seas were calm. I hadn't even noticed the roll of the boat before. But it does roll. Slowly left. Back to the middle. Slowly right.

Every time I open my eyes all there is to look at is the leaf-motif curtains which hang loosely from the bank of windows at the front of the cabin. And I watch these curtains intently. They don't move. But I can see the ship roll behind them. Slowly to the left. Back to the middle. Slowly to the right.

With each roll a new sensation invades my body. At first nausea then semi-paralysis. Then I am hit by the acute dreadfuls. Terminal confusion and gastro-interruptus — this is the state where you know you want to be sick, but you can't remember how to do it. Your innards have turned into one heaving, woeful blob of jelly. And you are stuck with it. It's the traveller's bonus written in small print, the near-death experience at no extra cost.

I'd swear I can see the grim reaper walking past. She is wearing a pink linen suit. I know this is an atypical outfit for the Angel of Death, but she has the right look on her face. And I am ready to kiss this hellish living-death of a seafarer's life goodbye.

I look across at my companion for reassurance. For help. Jan is so pale her freckles appear to be standing about ten centimetres above her face. But she can work her mouth.

'Next time,' she says. 'We swim.'

Then a new diabolical menace enters our lives. Group action. In the front left-hand corner — we are six rows back — someone throws up. Bags are provided. Then testifying to the credibility of the power of the domino theory and with the speed of a flame racing through gunpowder, seat by seat, row by row, passengers begin to throw up. And this psychological menace is running down the rows at breakneck speed towards us.

I look at Jan. She looks at me. And, with the threat a mere three upchucks away we bolt for the women's toilets. Jan, a latent athlete on land, becomes a champion sprinter at sea. She beats me in the door. Then I stub my toe on the doorstep on the way in, lunge through the doorway, skid on the accumulated slops and in what almost amounts to a backflip, land heavily on my coccyx.

I cannot tell you what relief we gained from throwing up. For there was none. NONE. You would be willing to throw up a kidney, two lungs and a spleen if it would help. But it doesn't. Seasickness is a blight of the brain. And your stomach remains suspended in confusion.

Having cleaned myself up with paper towels — a most unsatisfactory concept — we return to our seats to spend eternity and a half in an ashen-faced stupor waiting for morning.

At six o'clock the lights come on and passengers are cheerfully reminded that 'breakfast will be served in fifteen minutes'.

A collective moan issues from our weakened lips as one by one passengers stand up, stretch and hope for a new life.

Of course, there is that one bloke who leaps from his seat and exclaims, 'I'm really looking forward to some fried eggs,' and those of us around him deliver that I-hope-you-choke-on-them look while turning a greener shade of pale.

Jan and I, bedraggled and bemoaning, think we might improve our general state of wretchedness if we have some caffeine. Intravenously, if possible, or by cup. We feel our way down to the cafeteria where an unshaven chef whistles as he stirs the single pot on the stove.

'What would you girls like?' he asks, grinning. 'A stomach pump?' I fire a look of contempt at him which should have nailed him to the cabin wall.

'Geez, you two aren't exactly the life of the party, are ya? What d'ya want for breakfast? Some of this?'

'What is it?'

'Well, it's ya No. 1 dish there on the menu. See. Singapore Curry.'

I cannot begin to describe the gruesome nature of a pot full of Singapore Curry on this particular morning.

I look at Jan. Jan looks at me. And we bolt for the ladies toilets once more.

We lie dying for the final hour of the trip then wobble down the gangplank into Launceston ready to prostrate ourselves on the ground and give the earth a big hug. Our plan was to sit on a sea wall and look at the magnificent stillness of a fixed horizon, breathing in huge drafts of salty air as the sea gulls calked and cawed around us. Unfortunately, for another two hours our brains kept on rolling — slowly to the left, back to the middle and slowly to the right again.

Compared to the agony of the crossing, the rest of the holiday was blissful. We hitch-hiked around Tasmania from youth hostel to youth hostel. This accommodation proved to be historical and comic. One of the hostels required you to knock on a designated local's door to get the key. We did and we heard a woman shouting, 'Would you little buggers shut up ya yelling. There's someone at the door.' A woman opened the door with a runny-nosed baby on her hip. 'Ya've come for the key, have ya? Now that'll be six dollars for the night. Ya gotta fiddle the key to get it open. Ya turn the light on with the cord by the sink. And it's tank water. Don't waste it. And the dunny's out the back. And be careful when ya plug in the kettle. The switch is on the blink!'

The hostel consists of an old stone cottage, possibly built by convicts, with metal frame beds and stained horsehair mattresses. It was all charm and eerie history — the charm lay in the fact that a leg often fell off the chair as you went to sit on it and the eerie past was contained in the centimetres of dust on the bedside tables. The place seemed so right for an island where tragic history has unfolded and continues to unfold in settings of such dramatic beauty.

As for the dodgy plug, we only blew one kettle; it went off with a bang! Along with the lights. We had to use candles. When the young bikies who were camped by the river came up to say hello, I don't know who got more of a shock — them looking in the window at our spooky candle-lit faces or us looking out the windowpanes to to their hairy moon-lit mugs! They brought us some hot coffee. And when they found out we had no bathroom, they were willing to demonstrate the old army APC — armpits and crutch — routine in the river for us. But we felt our deodorant would see us through to the next day. And they went away.

Come to think of it, the only people we met on the trip were men. All the motorists who stopped to give us lifts were men. There was the Yugoslav in the Valiant who kept putting his hand on my thigh every time he changed gear on the column shift. I was, as I recall, sitting on the bench-seat next to him (the back seat being full of chickens in cages) and I was wearing a bathing suit at the time. I ticked him off. He pleaded ignorance of the language and changed gears an unnecessary number of times, I felt, on his way out of Hobart towards Port Arthur. Fuelled by indignant self-righteousness, I eventually demanded that he 'stop the car'. He did and we got out.

Other rides included trucks. One truckie took us out of his way to show us Zeehan, a virtual ghost town, which had become a rusting graveyard of mining machinery. Then there were the sales reps in station wagons. One was a speed pig. He drove up quietly enough, but as soon as we climbed in the car he slammed down the foot and took off. He'd whip around hairy bends on treacherous mountain roads and we'd end up sliding across the bench-seat nearly sitting on his lap. He thought it was a great joke but we wanted out. At the next town, he stopped for cigarettes — we got out.

There was another sales rep, 'I sell women's under-apparel. You would be a 34B.' He was right. We got a tour with commentary of the Queenstown area. 'Ya know girls, Queenstown had the copper mines. Sulphur was the problem. Killed everything. See. Bare mountains. Even the football oval. See. Gravel. They play footy with buckets of antiseptic around the oval 'cos they get so much gravel rash. It's a bloody shame really. It could 'a been a beautiful place.' He took us around the pubs. He took us around the churches. He was such a nice bloke and we didn't want to hurt his feelings (with his wife leaving him and everything), but we had to insist in the end that he let us out. He did. After another half-hour tour.

There were the medical students from Monash University. We ended up at a party at the Royal Hobart residents' quarters. We didn't have to pay for accommodation that night because we managed to party all night. But port and peanuts do not make the best meal combination. And we were a little limp-thumbed hitch-hiking the next day.

Then there was the local policeman from Campbell Town way.

'What are you girls doin' here?' he asked.

'We're just waiting for a lift. We're hitch-hiking around Tassie.'

'And how long 'ave ya been standing there?'

'At the Lake Leake turn off ... ooh about seven hours. And we've only seen two cars.'

'No bloody wonder. No one ever goes to Lake Leake. Come on. Get in. It'll be dark soon. I'll take ya to the next town.'

'Thanks.'

But always ahead of us was that dreaded return trip on the *Princess*. So terrified were we of the heaving, rolling *Princess*, if we could have exchanged our tickets for tickets on the *Titanic*, we would have willingly taken our chances. We had to help each other on board, we were so petrified. We didn't eat, we didn't drink. We sat up all night like two glass-eyed shop store dummies. And nothing happened. It was an uneventful trip.

We limped down the gangway into the passengers' lounge to be met by my parents.

'What are you doing here?'

'We've come to pick you up,' enthused my mother. 'Did you have a good trip?'

'Yeah. But what are you doing here?'

'Hello Mr Meehan. Mrs Meehan.'

'Hello Jan.'

'But what are you doing here?' I ask again.

'Two girls, hitch-hikers, have gone missing in New Zealand,' explained my mother. 'Your father was worried.'

'Oh Dad,' I sighed patting him on the head. 'You didn't have to worry. We know how to look after ourselves.'

THE COUNTRY TOWN

I'm in my early twenties. Every weekend is an adventure set between the inflexibile hours of the teaching routine. I ski. I canoe. I ride horses. It's mid-1970s and Australia is waking from a cultural slumber to embrace an entire world of new possibilities.

Italian restaurants open. And Greek. Wine sales soar. Women burn their bras. Rockfests boom and 'mystical happenings' happen.

We leave the city to ride bicycles through the foothills of the Great Dividing Range. And we discover little has changed in the heartland of rural Australia as we ride back, back in time, to the little Victorian country town of Daylesford.

It is summer. Birds call from the trees and the warm, languid wind billows softly over flaxen paddocks of uncut hay-grass. We push off, looking for adventure, full of the heady high spirits which come from inhaling strange substances, in this case fragrant country air. Unfortunately, when you are out of condition you do not get much mileage out of heady high spirits. In fact, you rarely survive the first uphill slog. After that it is hard work all the way, and even the best padded bicycle saddle soon offers little comfort.

We lose two of our party at the first signpost out of town. They decided to pedal back to their cars. The rest of us cycle on.

Daylesford, our destination for the night, is an old gold rush town which was originally laid out in much the same way as receding floodwater arranges debris along a river bank. There is little logic to it.

At the town limits we greet our advance party who drove there in their cars, and spent the afternoon wobbling around town on their brand-new Peugeot bicycles. They had become, apparently, quite overwhelmed by the ordeal. The two in question were young ladies of considerable refinement. They had both received a private school education. Their riding outfits were sporting and stylish, and brand-new from the bottom of their white shorts to the laces of their pale pink joggers. They had perfect suntans and amazingly long, elegant fingers. To cut a long story short, they were not used to hairy small-town yokels hanging out the windows of hotted-up FJ Holdens drooling, whistling and yelling, 'If you want it, come and get it.'

There was, alas, so little to do in town on a Saturday afternoon in the seventies that the young warriors of Daylesford cruised the main street in their mag-wheeled chariots, drinking beer and eye-balling the local talent.

Our advance party is so traumatised that, as soon as we arrive, they pack up their collapsible bicycles and head back to the big smoke. The rest of us limp and hobble towards the nearest pub.

It is a great old country pub; dark and musty inside even in summer. It has an old, creaky wooden staircase leading up to the residential section and an old red and black Persian-style carpet in the foyer and Ladies Lounge, which has obviously seen service in several Persian markets before making its way to Daylesford.

The entire hotel smells of stale beer, except in the women's lavatory where the pong of 'Lavender Bouquet' toilet deodorant could dissolve your adenoids.

By way of dressing for dinner, we wipe the dust off our sneakers and head for the 'lounge' where the sign promises 'counter teas'. The menu scribbled on a blackboard near the bar, offers: T-bone steak, roast beef, Chicken Maryland, and a mixed grill. The accompanying vegies consist of mushed peas and roast spuds, and there are mountains of coleslaw, big bowls of Three Bean Mix, and slices of beetroot dripping red juice, straight out of the tin. In other words, good old country pub fare.

The entertainment, however, is unique, even for a country pub. The local picture theatre had closed due to lack of custom, so, the owner of the pub, being something of an entrepreneur as publicans go, had decided to show a feature film in the Ladies Lounge, every second Saturday night, for the benefit of his clientele.

Oblivious of the treat that was in store for us, we work our way through a number of jugs of beer and assorted mixed drinks, place our meal order and sit around the table passing all manner of inane comment. Then a rather frail looking fellow staggers into the lounge lugging an assortment of film paraphernalia.

Various local chaps with wives or girlfriends in tow, sit in prime positions around the lounge eagerly anticipating the night's entertainment. They joke with each other and call to the projectionist.

'Come on Ted. Bring on the blue movies.'

'We won't be raided tonight Ted. The coppers have been called out of town.'

'Keep it above board, now Ted. No donkeys tonight, there are ladies present.'

'And a few donkeys.'

The locals laugh. They are keen all right, but no less keen than the gentlemen at our table whose eyes had lit up somewhat as they mumbled the likes of, 'This is a bit of bloody all right, isn't it?' despite the hostile glares of their female companions.

About five minutes after the slow hand-clapping commenced Ted stands in front of the home movie screen and calls for a 'bit of shoosh.'

'Ladies and gentlemen,' announces Ted amidst a tirade of cat calls.

'We couldn't get a feature tonight.'

'Boo. Hiss ...'

'Did the railway blokes knock off the reel again?'

'No. No. All we could get tonight were some shorts. But I'm sure you will find them ... ah ... entertaining.'

The lights dull. The projector rolls and just as I bite into my mixed grill I read the first title: *Install Your Own Comalco Aluminium Window Frames.*

You could have heard the thud as collective male chins in our party hit the table, but it was drowned out by the guffawing of the female members.

Now one would expect that such a film would only encourage conversation. No. Whenever we attempt to talk the locals shush us down. I learnt a good deal about aluminium window frames that night from a band of grinning overall-wearing tradesmen. I also learnt more than I probably needed to know about a yodelling tour of scenic Austria.

But the highlight of the evening hit the screen just as I get stuck into my fruit salad (Two Fruit with token cherry) dessert. The screen flickers, the strains of a Yugoslavian peasant polka fill the room as the film title rolls into place: *Your Daughter's Health* (circa 1948).

A stern-faced hospital matron comes into view, looks us straight in the eye and says the word 'hygiene'. We leave the lounge defeated. We trudge to our rooms past the football replay blasting in the bar, past the local lad relieving himself into the potted palm at the foot of the stairs and past the laundry which housed the publican's antique singlet collection.

We fall into our beds exhausted and go to sleep listening to the night sounds familiar to many country residents, of local louts doing wheelies up and down the main street.

THE CENTRE BY BUS

To appreciate the scale of Australia, to recognise its untameable vastness, do not fly to the centre of Australia, or drive your car. Take a bus.

I am a twenty-something career woman. The 1970s has opened a new panorama of possibilities. And I agree to a 7000-plus kilometre school trip by bus. I don't know what it is about blackboard chalk, but it must affect the brain cells.

And the bus driver we cop for this trip is three parts megalomaniac and one part bull terrier. As civilisation evaporates on the horizon, it becomes slowly apparent to the staff that we are not in control. The skinny, balding driver in regulation grey shorts and grey open-neck shirt assumes full command.

He assumes a lot of things. That young girls shouldn't read trash, for instance. He chucks the novels he disapproves of out of the bus window. Moreover, this megalomaniac has the overhead mirror, and he has the microphone. There is no toilet on the bus, so he has power over us. Bladder control.

Bored with the flat and open road, he looks in the mirror from time to time and says, 'Wake up everybody. Wake up. It's time for fun and games.' He is talking to a busload of Year 11 students, sixteen and seventeen-year-olds, as if they have been let out of a Home for the Lost and Bewildered for a day trip. There's a collective moan.

'Youse don't know what's good for yas. It's bloody boring out 'ere. Ya gotta make ya own fun.'

The teachers walk up and down the aisle whispering, 'Humour him.'

> There is no toilet on the bus, so he has power over us. Bladder control.

And so, with great reluctance, we play tear-a-kangaroo-out-of-newspaper. 'What are ya? Some sort of silly bugger. That's a boomerang. Well, wake up to ya self and listen next time, Missy... And I saw you down the back. Any more obscene kangaroos like that and you're off the bus, matey. I don't care if we're in the middle of bloody nowhere. You're off.' Pass the orange under your chin down the bus, then pass it back again: 'Nah. Ya buggers. Ya muckin' around. Ya didn't get it right. Ya gotta do it again.' Charades: 'Well one of yas must be able to do something. Don't they teach you anything at that bloody school of yours? How about one of the teachers? Yes. Give them a big round of applause boys and girls... Geez, they made a funny lookin' Abba. Three short arses and a bean pole.' And sing-a-longs: 'One man went to mow went to mow a meadow... I'm not bloody singin' this by meself ya know. Now join in. Two men went to mow went to mow a meadow... One man, two men and a dog... That's more like it... went to mow a meadow.'

The irony is, of course, the kids enjoy all of these escapades. It is the sabotage that keeps them entertained. Trying to muck up enough to send the bus driver off like a New Year's sky rocket. 'Jesus bloody Christ. You lot are hopeless. It's gonna take three weeks for that orange to get to the back at this rate. Now get your bloody act together. We'll start again.'

When we do stop for a toilet break, I learn a fundamental rule of the Australian outback. It does not avail itself as a suitable comfort stop for girls. The bus pulls to the side of the unmade rust-red road with Herr Megalomaniac calling the standard 'Boys to the left. Girls to the right.'

Now the boys, being typical of their kind, step off the bus and literally pee on the wheel. We teachers end up yelling, 'Move a bit further away boys. You're almost splashing our shoes.'

Meanwhile, the girls stand in a cluster on their side of the bus looking at a red dusty vision of treeless flatness stretching before them to the horizon. There is a lot of saltbush. Short, stumpy, twisted bushes of blue-green growing sparsely in the red earth. And that is it. Except for an outcrop of rocks dancing in a heat haze thirty kilometres away. There is nothing to hide behind. Nowhere to pee.

The girls head out into the desert and keep going. We staff stand by the bus yelling, 'That's far enough. Don't go any further girls. You might get lost. Come back.'

On we go for hour upon hour with the mesmerising drone of the bus wheels broken only when a road train, the huge desert transports, barrel down the highway towards us, rattling — it seems — every bolt and joint on the bus as it thunders past.

Apart from manic outbursts of torturous party games, we mostly pass thousands of kilometres in a trance-like state with the scene out the window merging into a characterless blur. Then suddenly we arrive with a flurry of excitement at some weird, mystical or bizarre destination.

Coober Pedy is weird. It looks like the film set for Moonscape III. The town is built on a barren white gravel plain which is now pock-marked with man-made craters and mounds from mine-shaft diggings. There isn't any grass. And no trees. Water is trucked in.

It is hot in Coober Pedy. So hot, in summer, you could bake an egg on your head if you stood still long enough. But it doesn't pay to stand still in Coober Pedy. It pays to dig. And the locals do. They dig for veins of opal. They dig into the chalky earth and make their homes underground.

Nothing in Coober Pedy is as it should be. People live in rabbit warrens. Rabbits are nowhere to be seen. Opals are everywhere and water is precious.

A special 'treat' has been arranged for the students. They are to sleep one night in a dugout in Coober Pedy. We staff — there are four of us — wisely choose to sleep above ground on the floorboards of the tin shed which protects the entrance of the dugout. It becomes a memorable night. Thanks to Casey.

Now Casey is a card. He is the sort of kid who would flick a rubber band and two times out of three hit himself in the eye. The other time he would hit the school principal. In Coober Pedy, Casey's feeling a little peckish so he buys himself a snack: one kilogram of dried apricots. Casey manages in one day to turn himself into Australia's greatest reserve of natural gas. And thirty-six kids sleeping elbow to elbow in sleeping bags in a one room dugout spend the night yelling, 'Casey. Cut it out.'

'Geez, Casey. Put a cork in it. MISS, can't you have Casey up there?'

Having thrown shoes at Casey all night, no one will sit beside him next day on the bus. After that, if Casey even looks at a packet of dried anything his mates throw him out of the shop.

✦ ✦ ✦ ✦ ✦

Ayers Rock — now Uluru — is all solemn myth and magic. This looming red monolith appears so out-of-context, it is easier to believe that it is, indeed, some monstrous red beast which has collapsed on the plain and might just rumble to life any minute, than to believe it is a benign lump of rock. And behind the rock is the searing blueness of the open desert sky. It's a giant postcard propped up in the desert.

On this trip we have every student type. The gigglers, the serious, the vague, the drama queens, the lazy, the depressed, the foolhardy. The lot. Then there is Lisa. Quiet Lisa. The Lisa who is no trouble at all, until it comes to climbing the rock.

She says nothing until she reaches the first pole that holds the chain guide running up the steep section of the rock. And there she freezes. Welded to the chain. Wooden. Unyielding. Nothing will shift her. We talk to her. Offer her drinks. Bribes. Threats. An hour later the teachers are trying to talk her down in shifts, but Lisa remains a fixture on the rock.

Then along comes John H. But John H. is an unlikely solution to the problem. Short and worldly, he swears and smokes. ('No smoking in the tents. Okay?' 'No worries, Miss.') He gambles. Poker is a favourite. ('John. I told you. No gambling.' 'Don't get in a flap, Miss. We're not gambling. Every twenty cents represents a match.')

He takes control. ('Piss off. I mean that nicely, Miss.') The next minute he is walking down the rock hand in hand with Lisa. I don't know what he whispered in her ear, but from then on smouldering looks flash across the bus. And I can't say the love was enduring. But I can say this, from that moment on Lisa was a new girl.

✈ ✈ ✈ ✈ ✈

Alice Springs is a comedy among the gum trees. We arrive in this oasis in the desert just in time for the Henley-on-Todd Regatta. This boat race is the perfect parody of the very formal Oxford Regatta — where young sporting men promenade in boaters and striped jackets with prissy young ladies of class — for formal, it isn't. Anything goes at a boating regatta where there is no water. Shorts and thongs are worn. Beer drunk from the can. And the boats picked up and carried in every race.

But there is something for everyone at the regatta. There are fishing competitions for the children. They have to dig fish out of the sandy bed of the dry Todd River. One of the races is called 'the Eights'. Eight team members run in line carrying a bottomless racing shell. And Surf Ski rescue. A lifesaver propels a wheeled surf ski along rails by paddling in the sand to save a young lady in distress. The young lady is a vital part of the proceedings as, apparently, the lifesavers wouldn't bother to rescue anyone else.

And the competitors are not at the peak of physical perfection — some of them must have cans prised out of their hands before the event. The regatta is a melodramatic spectacle of huffing, stumbling and swearing one-up-manship.

'Hey. You haven't got a bloody hope, ya wankers.'

'What a joke. You lot won't see us for dust, mate.'

What with the bush flies, dry heat, assorted folding aluminium picnic chairs, the burnt snag from the Rotary Club sausage sizzle, the local fire engine on display, a cold ale, fairy floss, being pressured into buying a ticket for the Lions Club spinning wheel, the Mothers' Club Devonshire Tea stall, the toffee apples at the church cake stall and kids chasing each other in and out of the crowd with the glee of the barefooted anarchy of the moment, the Henley-on-Todd is the classic Aussie day out.

✈ ✈ ✈ ✈ ✈

Meanwhile back at the caravan park I count forty-two coaches. At five in the morning you can't get a shower. We have to queue for the toilet. It is agony. And home never looked so good.

Yet so often this expedition through the centre turns up landscape features that are almost beyond description. How do you describe the weirdness of the Devil's Marbles, those red rocks playfully tumbled into place in the middle of nowhere, or the drama and stillness of the Olgas, that weirdly looming rock cluster, or the vitality echoing across the waters of Ormiston Gorge, a bizarre burst of life in the desert? Perhaps it is only the fantastic tales of weeping maidens and evil spirits of the Aboriginal Dreamtime that can do these features justice.

We drive on through the desert to Tennant Creek. Turn right. Drive another 1500 kilometres or so, to the coast. Townsville then Airlie Beach.

Travelling from the dry red centre to the tropics is almost an unbearable contrast for the senses. The warm, tropical air seems heavy and thick with moisture as it presses in upon us until beads of sweat form on our skin and trickle down our backs. The brilliant green lushness of vegetation seems precocious. And all the while the waves of the Pacific Ocean exhausted from crossing the Reef, gently roll on to the yellow bright sands of the nearby beach. It is paradise as I have always pictured it. Palm trees included.

We catch a thirty-six foot schooner at Airlie Beach to carry us to one of the uninhabited islands on the Barrier Reef for a night. On the way we snorkel a minor reef. Even underwater the tropics are brash and showy. The fish are swimming palates of fluorescent colour; the coral, explosions of electric pink, mauve and yellow; the reef, a pulsating kaleidoscope of colour and life.

The sky is an unyielding blue. The sea is as smooth as the skin on a jelly and the salty air touches our bare skin like a warm caress. It is a day of such tropical perfection, I can almost hear the tom toms calling. I am not alone.

First one kid, probably Casey, then another, dive into the water and start swimming for the island. In the end, they are all in. It is a vision straight out of adventures in paradise except for us teachers. We remain on deck busily counting heads. When they all make it ashore, we teachers quietly thank the gods of the high sea.

That night we sit around a bonfire on the beach telling tales of sailors' daring-do and treasure island stories. I watch the yellow light of the bonfire flames dance across youthful faces. Suddenly I realise the purpose of this expedition. The trip is not meant to teach the students history, geography, social science or geology. Though, miraculously, that can happen.

The purpose of the trip is to shake them out of their comfort zones and connect them to the world beyond themselves, to hook them on to life. And it works.

THE BUSHWALK

It is the duty of every Australian to don walking boots, a sensible hat, a checked shirt and a backpack and go bushwalking. At least once. If you live in the land of Oz you must, at some stage in your life, commune with nature, be one with the wilderness and sit on a stump sipping billy tea. And suck some pure and unadulterated eucalypt-rich bush essence into your lungs so that you can call yourself a fair dinkum Aussie.

Of course, you will also quite possibly enjoy huge blisters on your feet, aching joints and mossie bites the size of Everest. You get to inhale a few flies, remove the odd leech, eat charcoaled snags and sleep in a snug gully that turns, overnight, into a major river system capable of washing you out to sea.

As you may gather I do not harbour a great fondness for bushwalking. I love the bush. I just do not wish to go on the sort of holiday where you have to carry your kitchen on your back. But I have done my duty as an Australian. I first hit the bushwalking track in the 1970s when a backpack was a real backpack; a khaki canvas bag on a square aluminium frame; when an oilskin Japara was a real oilskin Japara (it had oil on it); and when the solitude of the wilderness called you (and no one else because no one had heard of a mobile phone back then).

I was blinded to the small discomforts and major agonies of the great outdoor experience because a new and mellow gooiness had enveloped my life. The Love/Lust Combo, that instantaneous lobotomy, that do-it-yourself hormonal imbalance, had swept me into a new frontier of irrational thought. The idea of wandering down a mountain track with the new-found object of my besotted affection whistling beside me, sounded alluringly romantic.

My HRH (His Royal Hyper-fitness; he could run two marathons a day, at the time) planned this trip.

Itinerary: Bushwalking.

Duration: Five days.

Location: Halls Gap, Victoria.

Participants: He, the fit twenty-something aesthete who enjoys long solitary walks in the bush to find peace and harmony. Me, the young girl who grew to womanhood in the bush, but had never actually walked in it.

> When I was a kid, hiking was pursued by yodelling Swiss health freaks or over-zealous scout leaders. Not normal people!

No one did. No one went bushwalking in the farming community I grew up in — not if they owned a ute or a Landrover or a motorbike. As far as anyone in the bush was concerned, when I was a kid, hiking was pursued by yodelling Swiss health freaks or over-zealous scout leaders. Not normal people!

HRH knew things about bushwalking. He'd heard of Paddy Pallin, the guru of bushwalking clobber and philosophy, when Paddy was still a lad, I think. So my beloved bought me a state-of-the-art backpack: khaki canvas with the aluminium frame.

I put it on and it felt about as comfortable as wearing a carthorse harness — not that I have donned a harness, but I suddenly found myself identifying with the oppressed cart-animal underclass. I would have called a draughthorse 'comrade' if I met one in the street. And all of this outpouring of emotion was triggered by the wearing of the empty pack. Incredulity was to follow.

We were to carry all the essentials. Food. Tents. Sleeping bags. Along with what I felt were my needs including several changes of clothes, two litres of Coke, a bottle of Bacardi Rum, deodorant (economy size), a good book, a pillow ('Why can't I have a pillow? What do you mean roll up your clothes? That would be so uncomfortable. You don't have to look like the grim reaper on vacation just because I mention the word pillow.'), bed socks ('It's autumn. I'll get cold feet.') and a police issue torch.

I wore walking boots. 'I feel like I've just joined the army,' I muttered. Then my beloved helped me into my backpack. I was shocked. Truly shocked. The pack was pulling me backwards. I thought the only way I would make any progress on this trip would be by stumbling backwards for the entire five days.

'I think I need less weight,' I said. 'I'll take out the Coke.' 'I'm carrying the Coke,' he replied. 'Oh. I'll take out the ... my ... um ... mascara then.' I left in my hairbrush, moisturiser, shampoo and conditioner. And we headed into the bush.

HRH had planned a short walk for the first day overland from Stawell to Halls Gap, only twenty kilometres. Before this walk, though I did indulge in infrequent outbursts of netball, my total walking experience did not exceed much further than Aisle 8 at the local supermarket. Twenty kilometres was further than I could imagine. But I suspected it would make a bloody long aisle at the supermarket. And I was right.

I would like to tell you about the extraordinarily sensual nature of walking in this magnificent location. We were heading towards the foot of the Grampians. Mysterious mountains, time-layered antiquity carved by the wind into dramatic rock-faced cliffs. We occasionally glimpsed these mountains as a blue-green haze on our horizon as we walked through flat grazing land. Then the horizon would vanish as we moved into corridors of eucalypt forests.

We saw so much local life. An echidna scampering across our track holding up her spiky skirt, running late for tea. A blue-tongued lizard with those ancient reptilian eyes merely flicking in recognition of our presence then ponderously turning to move on. Emus grazing on the flatlands like duel-handled mops with long necks. Wallabies drinking at a waterhole — dark, furred, dwarf-like creatures standing alert. Watching. Mostly watching. Then jumping back into the shadows of the forest in an instant as we moved closer.

We saw black cockatoos — majestic birds squabbling as if in some domestic fight in the tree tops. Spider webs — hundreds of spider webs beaded with dew and flung into trees like abandoned kites. One after the other. And there were the spiders. Blue and black horn-backed spiders sitting motionless mid-web surveying their domain.

I would like to tell more of these experiences, but I can't. By mid-morning I was having difficulty instructing my feet to walk. We stopped for an early lunch. When I tried to get up my legs weren't interested. They froze. I had to force them to straighten me up. We walked for several more hours then my legs seized up. Completely. I tried to sit down. But they wouldn't bend this time. I was walking like a tin soldier with rusted joints. We rested. It took me fifteen minutes to bend my legs. Then it was time to get up again. And they wouldn't straighten. And to be honest, I wasn't enjoying this experience.

Two hours later my mortal beloved made a noble gesture. 'I will carry your pack too,' he offered. 'How?' I asked. 'I'll carry your pack on the front and mine on the back,' he explained. 'And I'll carry the umbrella.' I had thought we might need it. He was still hoping we would keep to our schedule. On we trudged. One painful step at a time. On and on at dusk with bats, the little bush bats of the Australian bush, flitting in the moonlight between the trees. There was only one thought that kept me going. Hot water.

'If you can make it to Halls Gap we'll stay at the caravan park. You can have a hot shower.' The shower rose was, for me, the carrot at the end of the stick. I walked on counting each stiff, rickety step. One. Two. Three. Four. Rest. Hot Water. Go. Five. Six. Seven. Eight. Shower. Hot Shower. Go. Nine. Ten. All men are bastards. And over again.

We made it. We staggered out of the cold, dark night. Two shuffling cameos of miserable humanity. He put up the two-man tent while I showered. And showered. I dressed in slow, very slow, motion. Believe me, if I could have clambered back into my knickers without having to bend my legs I would have done it.

'This is so romantic,' I sneered back at the campsite, 'eating cold tuna from the can in the torchlight.' His hopes which flickered momentarily to life in his eyes at the mere mention of the word 'romantic' were soon reset on real-life probability as I mumbled, 'How am I going to get into the sleeping bag if I can't bend?' Adding as an afterthought, 'And it's all your fault, you bastard.'

He looked suitably chastened, but undaunted. There were, after all, four more days, and youthful lust burns like an eternal flame.

I struggled awkwardly into my sleeping bag and lay on the ground sheet without a mattress. His idea. 'Travel light' his motto, with my head on my rolled up coat, I felt about as comfortable as a roughly-felled log.

But I did sleep like a log too. Unfortunately, in the middle of the night I woke in fright. There was a roaring, groaning, hissing monster of a beast sniffing around our tent. 'Wake up,' I whispered shaking the sleeping lump beside me. 'There's a tiger outside the tent,' I hyperventilated. 'You're dreaming things. Go back to sleep,' he yawned. I lay there terrified. I heard what I heard. Then I heard it again.

'See? I wasn't making it up. It's a tiger.' 'Oh that,' he mumbled. 'It's just a koala. Go back to sleep.' He was snoring in seconds.

A koala? I'd seen plenty of koalas. Hundreds. The only difference between a real koala and a toy koala was geography. Neither moved.

I lay, log-like, listening to great roars and grunts waiting for huge claws to rip open the side of the tent to reveal savage salivating fangs just giving me enough time to scream, 'I told you it was a tiger,' before I was devoured whole in my sleeping bag like a human sausage roll.

It never happened. Dawn filtered slowly through the gloom. Magpies chortled in the nearby gum trees as the caravan park

The three wise koala's. Say nothin'. Think nothin'. Do nothin'.

environment slowly clattered back to life.

'Ah,' he said stretching and thumping his chest. 'We only have a short walk today, ten kilomtres.'

I gave him that look which suggested 'I'm seriously thinking of becoming an axe murderer. Would you mind fetching me an axe?'

'What's up?' he asked.

'I can't move.' I thought he'd have to stand me up like a bandaged mummy just to get me out of the sleeping bag.

'But I've mapped out the whole walk,' he insisted.

'Unmap it.'

'All right,' he replied. 'You don't have to get tetchy.'

'I'm not tetchy,' I snarled through gritted teeth. 'I'm a talking lump of wood.'

In the end, we compromised. I walked a few kilometres out of town with my head down — I didn't have the energy to hold it up. I must have looked like a dejected tin man hobbling along the yellow brick road. He plodded along with two packs and the umbrella. We camped by Lake Bellfield for four nights. On a slope. I remember it vividly. Our nylon sleeping bags slipped on the nylon ground sheet so that we woke every half hour with our feet sticking out of the tent. We then had to wriggle in our sleeping bags back into the tent like overgrown caterpillars. I was stiff in every joint including my teeth and I was not a happy little caterpillar at all.

That was my last bushwalking trip. I never went on another. And he never asked.

SAILING THE WHITSUNDAYS

Now married, our relationship survived the bushwalking fiasco. I had stated my case clearly to HRH. 'I will walk with you down the aisle. But no further.' There is, however, more than one way to strain the emotional bonds that tie us. Sailing together provides a particularly good method of testing a relationship as the only options available in a heated emotional crisis are sink, swim or stay on the boat. I have considered all three.

As you may recall I am a reluctant seafarer. I have no fondness for the sea when it is hurling me up and down and turning my insides out. But it is the 1980s and HRH (His Royal Heave-the-

Mainsail) is going through a spiritual phase of reconnecting with his inner nautical self. He has become a committed born-again sailor. And I went along for the ride.

I cannot say I am a worthy seafaring companion. My contribution to a day's boating is to drape myself over the gunwales and generally act as a form of human ballast while cheering on the frantic efforts of others. My boating expertise can be summarised as getting in the road, getting out of the road and looking innocent during crises.

Unfortunately we of the human ballast brigade, and there are a few of us about, occasionally fall victim to the wrath of the savage sea or the bile of an irate captain. We may not be seasoned sailors, but we've often been well-marinated bystanders.

My first recollection of yachting is of a one-week trip to that great inland sea in south-east Australia, the Gippsland Lakes, on board a friend's yacht. I would make more out of the fact that I know people who own a yacht, but Viking is an old wooden yacht of noble birth and cantankerous disposition.

Like many an old codger, it takes a good deal of effort to encourage the nearly eight metres of Viking to go where you want him to go and, like an irascible old-timer that he is, during exacting moments some vital bit is likely to drop off. Like the mast.

Not that any of this concerns me. I was just going on the trip to improve my suntan.

HRH (His Royal Horatio Hornblower) who always assumed command of any boat he sailed (even if made out of paper) insists that he has had extensive yachting experience and that I am therefore freed of the chains of anxiety which otherwise burden the inexperienced sailor.

Later, after head-butting a minor jetty with the nearly eight metres of keel boat and successfully running aground several times, I query HRH on the full extent of his yachting experience. He had, as he explained curtly, been a sea scout fifteen, or possibly, twenty years before this trip.

Anxiety would have set in at this stage but I am otherwise occupied seething with grievous outrage on discovering that I, the human ballast, am meant to do things on the boat.

This discovery is made during the procedure called CASTING OFF. I am told to cast off, so I mince up to the front of the boat and drop the mooring line while reading a magazine.

I do not know there is more than one mooring line. And I did not think I deserved the abuse hurled in my direction when we briefly motor in a short arc around the mooring pylon.

Having done my nautical duty I return to the gunwales to sunbake. This is when a certain degree of maritime friction ensues.

I want my companion to sail in straight lines so that I can bask in the comfort and warmth of the sun's direct rays, but he insists on tacking back and forth across the saltwater lake, so continually upsetting my equilibrium and casting me into mainsail shadow.

We cannot agree on the main priorities of the trip — my tan or responsible navigation — and when he does run a long reach for the benefits of my suntan we run aground and I am blamed. Eventually I decide I will put up with an anaemic tan and concentrate on reading books. Then I discover there is a more complicated procedure than CASTING OFF, known as ARRIVING. Or something like that.

I am sent to the front of the boat and told to jump on to the jetty with the rope and tie the aforementioned rope around a bollard.

And I have to do all this while the yacht is still moving, boats being sadly ill-equipped in the brake department.

As the boat glides towards the jetty, I poise myself for the jump. Two metres from the end of the jetty, I pounce. You may think I miss. Well, I don't. One foot lands on the jetty, the other foot misses.

I end up clinging to the edge of the jetty in what can only be described as the koala position. But I still hold the bow line. When I turn to note the position of the yacht I realise that several tonnes of keel boat are bearing down, bow first, on my shoulder blades.

This realisation spurs me on to greater efforts and I manage, using toe and finger nails, to claw my way on to the jetty and secure the boat.

By the end of the holiday I had stubbed my toe on every bollard and stay on the boat, I had tiller welts across my thigh, lower body wounds from slipping on the wet deck and upper body bruises from rolling off the bunk. And I had read only two chapters of *Mutiny on the Bounty*.

Despite several seasons of grumbling, complaining and sailing into emotional waters out of his depth, HRH gets an idea that we should sail the Whitsunday Passage, Queensland. Explore the Great Barrier Reef together. I agree. More sun, I think. This turns out to be a very stupid idea. As an ageing sea-scout and his innocent bikini clad companion, we could have been auditioning

> The dinghy fills with rain and sinks.
> It is wet. It is miserable.
> It is his idea.

for TV roles in a remake of 'Gilligan's Island'.

We hire a Holland 24 (a yacht) for the sound nautical reason that it has a double bed. This bed turns out to be in the bow of the boat. In other words, it was triangular. I don't know whether you've ever tried to sleep, or pursue other interests, in a triangular double bed, but the logistics of it are still a mystery to me.

After a short briefing from the boat-hire people we head off towards tropical islands with me lounging in bikini along the gunwales and HRH singing sea shanties at the tiller.

After a couple of hours the wind whips up and I withdraw to the cabin to read. An hour later the wind has become so fierce I find myself in wet-weather gear, life jacket and life line struggling with the tiller as HRH clambers towards the mast to drop the sails.

My eyes sting from the salt water, my fingers are numb with cold and the choppy sea is buffeting me around the cockpit. This, I say to myself, is not my idea of a tropical paradise. I could have stayed at home and been bruised for a quarter of the cost. But worse is to come.

The Holland 24, which has the overall appearance of a ten-man bathtub, has a design flaw. It does not have a topping lift. For those of you who, like myself, have taken very little interest in topping lifts, they are the wires which hold up the boom.

In a Holland 24, as the mainsail is dropped, the person holding the tiller is meant to hook the boom on to a backstay and all is well. Well, that is what HRH shouted at me across the gale as he bravely set forth in the storm to drop the mainsail. Unfortunately, whatever the plan was regarding the boom, I am not strong enough to hook anything anywhere. When the mainsail drops I am hit on the head by a collapsing high-speed boom, then buried beneath vast amounts of sail canvas. And I am the one steering this disaster.

HRH tethers himself to the stern and grabs the tiller out of my incompetent grasp. The sea is so rough I wasn't actually steering the boat anyway. Moreover, the tiller was steering me by tossing me back and forward across the cockpit. The light is fading fast. We struggle through a violent sea tossing us about like a white cork in a turbulent bowl of black ink to safe harbour at Nari Inlet.

We had, apparently, been enjoying the opening strains of a cyclone's opera. It takes me some time to recover from the trauma of this experience. My outlook on yachting doesn't improve until we are well into our second cask of wine.

We sit in Nari Inlet for five days looking out a leaking porthole at twenty other yachts as wind canon balls down the inlet walls and thuds into our rigging. Our yacht is dragged at anchor. The dinghy fills with rain and sinks. It is wet. It is miserable. It is his idea. And we are waterlogged, unhappy, and marooned in Nari Inlet.

The thing about Nari Inlet is that it's next to perfect. Perfect is the next inlet. Nari, once a little piece of paradise, all stone canyon walls and tropical forest, has been turned into a subway. Graffitied. Boating folk carry cans of paint up the canyon walls to graffiti this patch of tropical paradise with boat names and incidental thoughts. Guncat. Miss Louise. Wind Dancer. They are all there.

For five days I sit looking out the porthole at a one-metre-tall red slogan. Jesus Lives. And I'm sitting there, thinking mean and nasty thoughts about the graffiti artist. I'm sort of hoping he fell down the canyon wall and ended up living with Jesus.

When the weather clears I think it is heaven. If Jesus does live here, he's picked the right spot. We're surrounded by dreamy turquoise-crystal seas and lush tropical islands heaped with coral sands. I spend several hours at the bow of the yacht trying to catch electric-blue and black Dunk Island butterflies in my discarded pantihose. Whoever has a butterfly net when they need one? But I still bear emotional scars from the trip.

So,
You can drink to your weekend-sailors, me boys
and drink to the treacherous tide
but I drink to the unsung heroes, me boys
to folk who just go for the ride.

SURFERS WITH THE KIDS

The wheel of life has turned. It is the early 1990s. HRH and I have two children, an overdraft and a station wagon. We are turning into a statistician's demographic group. We live by the rules of suburbia. Garbage Sunday. School Monday. Piano Tuesday. Guitar Wednesday. Tennis Thursday. Takeaway Friday. Runaround Saturday. Repeat.

And the pressure is on. There is an unwritten rule of suburbia. Kids know it. Parents know it. You are not a fit and decent parent unless you take your children, at some stage in their lives, to the theme park capital of the world. Surfers Paradise.

We do it. We take our children to kid heaven. To Australia's Tourist mecca. We go north. To Queensland. To Dream World. Sea World. The Big Pineapple. The Big Macadamia Nut. After three days I started looking for the attraction known as The Big Sedative Tablet.

I am, in fact, typing this with a pencil in my mouth. They tell me I won't get out of the straightjacket for two weeks — not until I stop twitching. And please, don't mention the word rollercoaster in my presence. My eyeballs go out of control and start rolling around in my head. And if I see another dolphin, I swear, I will ... I will lock myself in the bathroom and take an overdose of raw mullet.

I am the victim of a condition known as Theme Park Stress. Many, many parents suffer from this tragic complaint. It all begins at Sea World. Sea World is a fantastic place, which explains why three billion other people decide to visit Sea World on the same day as us. Well, that's what it feels like.

We have to queue for forty-five minutes for the Bermuda Triangle ride. The ride is brilliant. But the queue was very spooky. The Bermuda Rectangle, I called it. I could believe that entire busloads of people have disappeared without trace in that shuffling queue. We are lucky to survive.

The rollercoaster is similar. We wait twenty-five minutes for a thirty-second ride. It is over so quickly we don't know if we've been on it or not. I suspect they just load you in one side of the rollercoaster and out the other. There is a similar wait on the water slides. As one of my kids explains, 'When you say goodbye to the kid next to you in the queue, you feel as if you are sort of leaving a lifelong friend.'

The rides contribute to my stress levels. 'Come on Mum. You'll love it,' the kids yell happily at each ride-on instrument of torture. On the Corkscrew Rollercoaster, I feel as if I am being spun dry on the heavy duty cycle. I suspect I am four centimetres shorter after this ride. During the Thunderbolt Rollercoaster ride — with the two loops — I feel my jowls pinning me to the back of the headrest. I think I will have to step off the rollercoaster carrying my cheeks in my hands. But the Gravitron, at Dream World, gives me the biggest thrill. As it starts to spin, I see some things fly either side of my face and hit the wall. My boobs. I swear. I thought I would have to wheel my bustline out of the Gravitron in a wheelbarrow.

But the real cause of Theme Park Stress for parents is their children. This trip costs big smackeroos. We spend enough money on the trip to put a small kingdom on lay-by. It is not my idea of a holiday. My idea of a holiday is to lie inert by a heated swimming pool sipping a cocktail sporting little umbrellas while being massaged by the cast of Under Siege II. Or something like that. But we did it for the children.

And I expected them to walk into each of these worlds radiating an ambient glow of gratitude. But they didn't. They argued over whose turn it was to sit in the front of the Viking Ship, Imitation Log, or the mine trolley. And I found myself saying things like, 'For God's sake Indiana Jones did not care if he sat in the front or the back of the mine trolley. Now get in.'

Since then, I have discovered that Theme Park Stress is quite common. One friend explained that her kids grizzled on to the plane, grizzled off the plane, moaned on the bus and when they arrived at Movie World the youngest one became hysterical. Bugs Bunny was SO BIG. He was a good two metres tall. He's only ten centimetres long on telly. The little one screamed and wouldn't let go of her mother's neck for the next four hours. 'And we payed for this torture,' sobbed my friend.

So there it is. If you are going to take your children to a theme park, train for it. Do deep breathing exercises hanging upside down from the monkey bars. Try meditation while bouncing on a trampoline. Do yoga sitting on top of a pineapple. Then and only then will you be able to combat Theme Park Stress.

Alternatively, you can wait with me until they open a theme park called No Whinge World. Now that would be something.

TWO
THIS TRAVELLING LIFE
or How to Organise the Mid-life Crisis For Fun and Profit

ANYWHERE IS GOOD AT THIS TIME OF THE YEAR!

I was sitting down one overcast Saturday afternoon calmly planning my mid-life crisis when the realisation struck me: 'There is a serious shortage of viable mid-life crisis options for a girl.' What's a girl of a certain age to do?

I could get a tattoo of a rose on my bum, but I couldn't stand watching its little petals wilt over the years.

I could run off with a younger man. But there being a world shortage of smouldering young Latino lovers who can massage feet, cook a Thai stir-fry, vacuum clean, and unpack the supermarket shopping at the same time, I felt the odds were against me.

I could join a religious cult, but these cult leaders all seem to have graduated from the Charles Manson School of Charisma. One minute you are heading off for a good day out at the annual cult picnic, and the next minute you find you have front row seats at the mass suicide.

Quite possible... YOU ARE HERE!

I could dance naked around an elm-wood bonfire at the full moon to the beat of a home-made tom tom to get in touch with my inner she-devil. But this would strike terror into the heart of my neighbours, and my family would simply assume I'd finally made complete and irreversible contact with my inner psychopath. No doubt they would promptly pack me off in a pink dressing gown to a Home for the Dearly Demented.

I could go for the born-again-Barbie-doll look; get the boob job, the nose job, the bum job, pump up the lips, pump the cellulite out of the thighs, tizz the hair, load up on gold jewellery to go with the short shorts, midriff top and high heels. And I know what I'd look like. Nip 'n Tuck Barbie; the Barbie doll with the smile that meets at the back of her head, and with ballistic boobs worn tragically at her waist.

I could wipe the slate clean. Go for a divorce. Divide the assets. Sell the house. Oh hell! I'd have to clean it first. You can forget that little idea. No way is my mid-life crisis involving any housework in any form. I've done enough of that already.

I could buy an old sports car, and relive the image of a scarf-wearing Grace Kelly cruising the clifftop of Monaco with Cary Grant in the car. And where would I be driving this erotic fantasy on wheels? To the supermarket. Ahhh! I don't know. The image doesn't work for me. Sitting next to Cary Grant holding bag-loads of Corn Flakes and two-ply toilet tissue loses some of the erotic feel in translation.

I could become an alcoholic. Sometimes, slapping on the lipstick in that mad dash out the door, I miss my mouth by about a centimetre, and arrive at a social gathering already looking like an alcoholic long before I've even managed to rugby-tackle a passing waiter to get a drink. But, tragically, my taste in wine has moved steadily upmarket to the point where, even if the oblivion of alcoholism held appeal, I can no longer afford it.

But I still had the nagging feeling that something was missing in my life.

What?

I've always dreamed of taking a slow boat to China, but I seem to spend most of my life in the fast lane with a supermarket trolley.

That's when I was struck in a blinding flash with a brilliant idea. I should travel. I should pack up my mid-life crisis, shove it any-old-how into my bum bag, and go! Forget the mortgage. Take the kids, or maybe leave the kids? Pack as many of my insipid credit cards as I can fit into my wallet, and, where needs be, throw in my mortal beloved and his more-than-useful stack of heavy duty credit cards. And go!

Travel, travel, travel

And write. I shall become a travel writer.

I shall sail the seven seas, if there are still seven seas left to sail. I shall climb every mountain, ford every stream, follow every rainbow and, if I'm not careful, morph into Julie Andrews before the year is out and start running around the Austrian Alps in a peasant skirt.

I shall travel. I shall travel and share my mid-life crisis with the world. But where on this vast and untamed planet will I go? It doesn't matter. To me, anywhere is good at this time of the year as long as the destination includes accommodation I don't have to vac.

ZEN and The Art of Drinking Chianti on a Terrace in Tuscany

Before we go on any adventures together, dear reader, there are certain clauses in my contract as a travel writer to which I believe I should draw your attention.

Clause 23.11

I, your intrepid travel writer, to wit myself, have no intention of engaging in any of the following travel experiences for the purposes of writing a book:

- I have no intention of being kidnapped by highland tribesmen and being held to ransom in a bark hut (with live-in parasites) for three fattened pigs in some politically unsettled region.
- I have no desire to catch malaria, typhus or the Black Death (it's regaining popularity in some regions), or suffer from any

- form of dysentery, to add pathos and drama to the travelling experience, as I see no future in travel writing if compelled to return home as ashes in the post.
- I have no intention of being attacked by a wild boar, gored by a gazelle, mauled by a grizzly bear, or even rattled at by a rattlesnake. I will be standing on the right side of the safety fence at all times and on all occasions, including watching the Queen (though I do believe she is harmless at close range).
- I have no intention of getting tangled up in a small-scale civil war, popular uprising or unscheduled *coup d'état* anywhere in the world, despite the photographic opportunities, as I have no interest in experiencing a free ride in a United Nations helicopter or acquiring a genuine bullet-riddled blood-stained T-shirt momento when I'm providing the blood.
- I will not eat fresh monkey brains straight out of the skull or even out of the handy takeaway pack, nor am I interested in eating anything raw that has not yet acquired the fully deceased — and well-marinated — state.
- I will not whitewater raft the Amazon, as I have no fondness for leeches, piranhas, or writing underwater while drowning.

That said, I realise that basically, I your travel writer, am committing myself to day after day of sitting on a sun-drenched terrace overlooking a hazy-blue valley in Tuscany, while sipping chianti and listening to Pavarotti on an especially fine stereo system. But I want you to know that I will be tirelessly taking notes, that I will pursue my obligations with a passion, with gusto, with flair and grace, and with a selfless dedication above and beyond the call of duty. And I will do it, dear reader, entirely on your behalf.

GEOGRAPHY and Why I Should Have Paid More Attention in Class

Having embraced travel as the new frontier of my life plan, I had to spin the globe and pick a destination. I don't know if I should be telling you this, but when I stopped to muster the full weight of my knowledge of geography for this purpose, I found my information banks sadly lacking.

The only geography I remember learning at school involved little plastic templates that we had to draw around and colour in. I owned Australia and Victoria. My mum bought them for me. And I loved colouring a blue fringe of sea with a Derwent pencil around the carefully traced-out map. Of course, I never knew which sea I was colouring in. But I was pretty sure it was blue. And that sums up my school-based knowledge of Australian geography.

When I tried to conjure up an informed vision of Europe all I could scrape out of the memory banks were random sketches of Big Ben, the Eiffel Tower and the Colosseum accompanied by the school chant that goes: 'Long-legged Italy, kicked poor Sicily and made poor Malta hop.' Otherwise Europe consisted in my mind of a collage of pink, green and yellow bits in an old school atlas.

I could recall that there were things known as wheatbelts in America and that 'Wheat is a cereal grain (closely related to barley and rye) which constitutes the chief breadstuff in temperate countries' and this would make, as far as I was concerned, a rather useless belt.

Otherwise my knowledge of American geography has come to me through popular songs. I'd know where to go in America. I'd have to: 'give my regards to Broadway'; 'cross the wide Missouri'; visit Minneapolis in the summertime because 'God didn't make little green apples and it don't rain in Minneapolis in the summertime'; spend some time 'under the boardwalk down by the sea', a peaceful afternoon 'sitting at the dock of the bay' or 'up on the roof' or 'laying on Arkansas grass' and I'd have to find out what Billy Joe Macalister and that girl threw off the Telahasee bridge. I may not know much about the rest of the world, but I could hum my way around America blindfolded.

With an obvious need to broaden my travel knowledge base, I started collecting travel brochures. That's when I discovered the dastardly disease which, sadly, affects nine out of ten travel brochure writers: cliché gibber-itis. The truth may be out there somewhere, but it rarely makes an appearance on a typical travel brochure.

You can't just go to the tropics. In travel brochure land you 'visit the tropical paradise of your dreams and let the gentle breeze of friendliness wash over you'. You can't just wander around the Alps. In travel brochure world you 'gaze upon the enigmatic mountains and stroll among the hidden vales and moss-laden arbours of timeless beauty'. I decided travel brochures were of little value to the inexperienced traveller. It was too difficult to decide which overly florid or unbearably cute cliché in the world to visit.

I tried reading travel articles in newspapers and travel magazines. They were no help. I wanted to go everywhere. The *Golfo dei Poeti* (The Gulf of Poets), Italy; Key Largo, Florida; the hidden city of Sikkim, Tibet; The Mull of Kintyre, Scotland; Ocho Rios, Jamaica; The Matterhorn in the Swiss Alps; Mumbai, wherever it is, and all on the QE2.

I talked to friends. Some of their recommendations could have been pooled to create a new travel concept: Death Wish Tours. I'd mention the word travel and these friends would plunge instantly into a dreamlike trance recalling some youthful adventure in a flower-painted Kombi van in the seventies through bizarre locations, which were truly exotic and cheap three revolutions ago, but could now include, for unwary Westerners, a ritual beheading at no extra cost.

Other friends offered basic business trip advice, namely 'How to remember, when you wake up in your five-star hotel, which country you are in' and 'How to fit (into a full schedule) a visit to the Great Wall of China in three and a half minutes' — all expenses paid, of course.

In other words, the travel advice offered by friends was about as useful to me as trying to book the next tornado in Kansas for a Dorothy-like tour of Oz.

But finally it was decided. We would pack all of our emotional eggs in one touring basket and travel to our ancestral homelands, our personal holy lands (Monet's garden in Giverny, France, held significance for my family) and visit our long-lost relatives all in one trip. We would do Europe or, at least, the pink, green and yellow bits.

MS WEREWOLF IN LONDON

So this was it. The big trip. I, who had aspired to travel all my life, reached for my passport, searched for my passport, turned the house upside-down looking for my passport to discover, finally, after digging it out from the tangle of pantihose at the bottom of my undies drawer, that it was dead. Caput. Finito.

The one stamp in the now-deceased passport recorded a manic two-week tour of the United States of America ten years before. On the scale of life's fun experiences, however, this sojourn ranked right down there with the annual trip to the gynaecologist. I was in my mid-thirties, pregnant with a bad back and accompanied by a four-year-old. What I remember most clearly about that trip is that I could have checked my boobs in as excess baggage. That sums up my complete world travel experience in the eighties.

The only other overseas adventure I'd managed was a mad dash around Europe, during the Australian school holidays, in the seventies. In other words, I had spent most of my travelling life at home. But that state of concrete inertia was about to be blown out of the water by my mid-life mania.

But first I needed a new passport. This was the *bon voyage* shower tea, with red tape, you experience before you leave. I stood in my local Quick Pix shop trying to look like a glamorous international traveller rather than an alcoholic — I had missed my mouth with the lipstick again — while a fifteen-year-old girl who was paying careful attention to hairy-legged schoolboys outside the window, snapped my passport photograph.

Have you noticed how work ID photographers, motor licence phototakers and passport-shot snappers have all graduated from the Boris Karloff school of photography? We are talking horror shots. It seems to be a requirement of the work ID photograph that your eyes must be sufficiently out of whack to make you look like the complete spaced-out junkie — whacko, as well as incompetent. I don't know why it doesn't worry more employers that they are surrounded by work IDs that suggest the majority of their staff should be on the methadone programme.

Motor-licence photographers try to produce a photograph that suggests you are the product of a long line of in-breeding, and your mother was a werewolf. The advantage is, of course, when

Open at own risk

that police officer asks for your licence, he may run off screaming.

Passport photographers try to add a little interest to your overseas travels by taking the sort of photograph that suggests you are a long-time resident of Australia's Most Wanted List, or have undergone a recent autopsy.

When I had my passport photograph taken, I got the ID-combo and came out looking like Australia's Most-Wanted Werewolf Drug Addict. True! And you get four of these photographs, as if one isn't traumatic enough! But I'm not alone.

I bring you this quote from the *Evening Mail*, a newspaper in Scotland:

> Interviewed after his release by the Austrian Border Police, Mr John Louvet, an investigative journalist, agreed that he had been travelling throughout Europe with a snap of his neighbour's cocker spaniel 'Chummy' as his passport photograph. A police spokesman said, 'It was a very good likeness.'

You can see what's happening can't you? There has been a major international computer virus affecting the passport office, and a number of us have ended up with Chummy's photo on our passports. Meanwhile, if a customs officer orders me to 'sit', I can't decide if I should simply comply or fulfil the expectations of my passport photograph and bite him on the ankle!

The next step in acquiring an Australian passport involves knowing people in high places, so that these dignitaries can verify that you are who you say you are — as this is in doubt, due to the fact that you only seem to be able to locate your birth certificate, marriage certificate, Year 12 graduation certificate, university degrees, overdrawn bank accounts, a tax file number, a Medicare number, a licence number, and a membership number for the Omo-matic Suds Club — and that you are indeed as ugly as your photograph suggests. And pay a fee!

These dignitaries include accountants, dentists, doctors, vets, pharmacists, police officers, teachers and nurses. If you are a healthy, law-abiding citizen who does her own tax return and doesn't own a pet, you are left with the prospect of having to go back to your Grade 4 teacher, Mrs Fitzgerald, saying, 'Remember me? Without the pigtails!'

At least, I have now found a reason for going to university. It didn't guarantee me a career. It didn't broaden my understanding of life, the universe, or radio-alarm clocks. It didn't even teach me how to use a pocket calculator, due to the tragic fact that they hadn't been invented then. What university training furnished me with, however, was a trusty band of rag-tag friends who are now sufficiently elevated in society to sign a passport application form. I can remember many a sobriety-deprived night with such friends, and I never thought they would rise to such noble heights.

Dignitary's signature in place, I attended an interview with the local post-office manager to answer questions such as, 'Do you like our Christmas decorations?' I was a little worried that it may be a trick question. Was it a test to see if I could be safely let out of Australia? Should I say, 'No. I would like something with a more global-friendly theme. Perhaps Santa could do a Jamaican thing — dreadlocks, multicoloured suit, up-tempo music, and the sleigh could be pulled by a team of endangered species led by Rudolph the Red-nosed Numbat?' But, in the end, I went for the typical Aussie answer. 'Yeah. They're all right.' And it worked. The manager took my application form and sent it off to bureaucrat city.

Phase three of obtaining my passport involved turning up at the passport office some weeks later, collecting a number and waiting. And waiting. I was beginning to believe that my new passport would mature, ripen and expire before I got it. But, hooray, at last my number was called. I bounded into a booth. And sat there waiting. And waiting. Finally someone wandered past the booth and asked me what I wanted.

My immediate thoughts were, 'I am sitting in the passport office. What do I want? A facial and a full body massage? What do you think?' I thought it, but I didn't say it. Passport people have passport power. They may be able to encrypt a secret code on my passport suggesting I am 'Mrs Day of the Jackal' or something.

I smiled. I tried to fake a stroke so that I would look like my passport photograph, and eventually I was handed a little blue book with a gold kangaroo and emu on the cover and my name in the front.

And, in the very front of the passport, the Queen, her good self, has requested 'all those whom it may concern to allow the bearer to pass freely without let or hindrance and to afford him or her every assistance and protection of which he or she may stand in need'. How's that? The Queen wants everyone in the world to look after me. I think the first thing I'll do in London is drop in on Buckingham Palace 'without let or hindrance' for a cuppa. I mean, the Queen wouldn't put that in the front of every one of our passports if she didn't mean it.

HOW TO AVOID BEING MISTAKEN FOR A COLUMBIAN DRUG LORD and Other Handy Travel Hints

The next phase of the travel experience demands the sort of organisational skills required to stage-manage the D-Day invasion of Normandy. You need maps, guidebooks, train, plane and bus timetables, a moderate grasp of ticket reading skills in several languages, and a workable knowledge of time zone and daylight-saving factors so that the entire itinerary doesn't collapse in a pathetic heap at the first stop.

The keystone to this orchestration of a personal world event is the guidebook. It can tell you how to book into a hotel, how to buy theatre tickets and how many years it will take you to get to the airport in peak hour traffic on public transport. A guidebook can walk you in 3-D cutaway detail through the Seven Wonders of the World, or lead you to what turns out to be the Eighth Wonder of the World in a time of need — the nearest public toilet.

So precious is this information, you cling to the guidebook even as you walk through foreign streets. And though it may, at times, broadcast the fact that you are indeed a suitable person to overcharge, rob or ignore, you still need it because it gives you the sort of confidence which says, 'I may look lost to you but I know exactly where I am. I'm somewhere in this book.'

✈ ✈ ✈ ✈ ✈

As you flick through a guidebook to any country, a European destination for instance, the clichés roll off the page with a comfortable familiarity. You make a note of the picturesque tree-lined *straats*, the local Renaissance-style *kathedraal*, the must-see *Musée d'Art*, the significant 12th century *abbaye*, the Roman foundations of the nearby *kasteel* walls, and the ornate stone canopy of almost anything. But little is said of the minutiae of the travelling life.

The sort of information that travellers need to know and guidebooks blatantly suppress such as:

- How to say 'No suppositories' to a pharmacist in French.
- How to purchase, with some dignity, a sticking plaster in the Netherlands when 'Band Aide' means Female Hygiene Product.
- How to fill in a night on the depressing fringes of Calais, which the Allies bombed during the war, marking the last exciting night out anyone had in Calais.

So, to help you read between the lines of any reputable guidebook, I offer, through the benefit of hindsight, these additional notes.

1 Transfers included

This means you will be whisked instantly from the airport to your hotel while being plied with French champagne in the back of the stretch limousine. You will be carried to your room along with your luggage by a cheerful, tip-refusing porter. The other 99 times out of 100 it means you will have to rugby-tackle a passing transfer agent to secure your place on an over-crowded mini-bus, which (after a two-hour wait at a fume-soaked transfer point) will take you directly to your hotel with a small detour to drop thirty-eight passengers off at their hotels first.

2 The three-star hotel

The three-star hotel may be a refurbished 17th century *chateau* which provides you with a comfortable room and *en suite* charmingly installed by a pre-Renaissance plumber. More often than not, the three-star hotel is a three-storey post-modern shoebox. The *en suite* is so compact you sit on the toilet with your feet in the bath and vice versa. And in the middle of the night you discover your hotel is currently hosting the Bulgarian Door Slamming National trials.

3 Phrase book

The standard, compact, easy-to-use phrase book enables you to say — by the cunning use of kindergarten phonetics — the likes of, 'Can you help me? My stopcock is broken,' in Dutch. It does not require, however, brains much bigger than a remedial mole to realise that the person to whom you direct your question will reply at three billion words per minute in their native tongue, which you will not — even given three weeks to translate — understand. Consequently, you will be left standing in a public place looking like a total idiot holding a broken stopcock.

4 Laundry available

The problem is the word 'laundry'. It means different things in different places. In the Netherlands, laundry means 'take these twenty-nine separate washing potions and conditioners, put them into this industrial-strength decompression chamber with the heavy duty cycle and pound the living daylights out of your underpants for the next two hours until clean'. If your underpants make it to Switzerland you can have them washed, pressed, packaged and returned for the same cost of flying them to Australia and back first-class to be washed by your mum.

And this is one tip you will not read in the guidebook.

If unsure of laundry facilities, always take your mum with you!

5 Airport security

Airport security is there, as you know, to separate the likes of homicidal psychotics on inadequate medication, militant terrorists on suicide missions, and mob hitmen on a working vacation, from the rest of us. As a noble citizen of the world, you go through the screening station like a robot pre-set on security screen mode.

Drop luggage. Walk through screen frame. Wait for personal scan. Collect luggage. You don't even think about it.

It therefore comes as a complete and unexpected jolt to your complacency when a heinous fiend is nabbed at some foreign airport right under your very nose and it turns out to be you. Tragically, trying to prove your innocence in a foreign language will only confirm the authority's assessment of you as the desperation in your voice will link you directly to one of the more colourful classes of maniac.

To avoid ending up sealed in some airless, windowless interview room seated opposite a hard-faced interrogator who shares only one word in common with you, namely 'Baywatch', while trying to recall your maternal grandmother's maiden name to prove that you are indeed who you say you are, and that you are also a humble, law-abiding citizen despite the blood-soaked, bullet-holed 'I got wasted in Chicago but you shoulda seen the other guy' T-shirt in your luggage, you must observe airport etiquette.

Do not carry in your hand luggage:

- A souvenir cheese knife (being bent at the end it is assumed this knife is very dangerous because it can stab around corners).
- A bullet key ring (security may spend five hours looking for the gun).
- A hand grenade cigarette lighter (and if you are stopped carrying such an item, for God's sake, don't try and demonstrate that it is just a cigarette lighter, you'll very likely be shot before you can pull the ring).
- A ceremonial dirk or sword (in some countries you may be expected to commit ritual suicide on your arrest).
- A thermos with a cute little radioactive symbol on the lid.

In addition:

- Make sure your camera tripod does not look like an easy-to-assemble assault rifle on the X-ray.
- Do not look like Carlos, the terrorist.
- If your initials are IRA, change your name.
- If the alarms go off as you walk through a security screen reach for the change in your pocket slowly. If your money clip has set off the alarms, take the money out of the clip and hold up the clip for inspection. If you merely hold up the money in the clip — this is what my beloved did at Singapore Airport — you will be grabbed under the armpits by two machine gun-toting airport security officers and dragged to the aforementioned airless interview room for attempting to bribe police, and much talking will be required to avoid dire consequences.

6 Leisure or tourist map

All right, you can deal with the roads they forgot to mark and the freeways that haven't been added yet and the fact that you are travelling to a town ten centimetres off the map. The real problem with tourist maps is they do not include cars, trucks or roadworks. This is misleading. You may plan to pop across from Antwerp to Eindhoven for a couple of hours. It is after all only a two-centimetre trip on the map. It takes you two days to travel one centimtre and, at one point, it appears that you will spend the rest of your life on the Eindhoven ring road system in holiday traffic. However, you can spend this time well by plotting to rid the world of the tragic pestilence known as cartographers.

7 The major tourist attraction

The problem is that major tourist attractions, not surprisingly, attract tourists. Millions of them.

Think of the French Revolution. Think of the rabble and the storming of the Bastille. Now, this is the Eiffel Tower on a good day. On a bad day, if you don't pass out in the queue from malnutrition or sunstroke, you will end up packed in the lift with a group of American tourists receiving electric shock therapy from the constant rubbing together of their polyester outfits. Try minor tourist attractions.

See less and live longer.

8 *La toilettes automatique*

These French-designed automatic toilets, which look like silver single-seater telephone booths, can be found dotted all over Europe. Don't trust them. The French have not recovered yet from their success with the guillotine. If you are slow, those automatic doors could take off your leg. The auto-flush means you may enjoy an unscheduled bidet-experience. While those a little slow leaving may experience an unscheduled fully-clothed shower as the auto-dunny automatically sanitises itself.

Then, on the other hand, if you are desperate and hopping around on one foot outside Notre Dame, what's your choice?

It's any pot in a storm!

9 Customs

In many airports a yawning customs officer will simply wave you through the customs station without so much as a simple peek inside your luggage.

At other airports the term 'customs' means 'strange customs and bizarre rituals conducted at this point'. This includes having your dirty underpants inspected by a panel of three judges, having a souvenir sex toy arranged in public display for the entertainment of the passers-by and having any contraceptive devices inspected as if the customs officer was just handed a 'Solve This 3-D Puzzle Fun Pack'.

To avoid being mistakenly arrested as a suspected drug courier, exotic bird smuggler or an international art thief — adding to your trip the interesting experience of being strip searched and dosed with suppositories before being thrown into a flea-ridden penal institution to await trial in a foreign language — certain rules of touring must be observed while negotiating customs.

Do not pat the sniffer dog.
Do not talk to your luggage.

- Do not fill your shoes with excessive deodorant powder and/or carry this powder about your person in small plastic bags.
- Do not twitch or show any other signs of possible drug use, for example reciting erotic Sanskrit poems to a potted palm in the transit lounge.
- Do not pat the sniffer dog. Because he has few friends, he may not leave you alone.
- Do not talk to your luggage.
- Look friendly. But not too friendly — in some countries a smile may be interpreted by a bald, sweating and swarthy middle-aged customs official as a request for sexual favours.
- Make sure the souvenir grass skirt you bought in the back street bazaar was designed to be worn and not inhaled in some form.
- Do not carry sticks of Blu-Tack in your hand luggage. Even United States customs officials prefer to suspect you intend to blow up the Golden Gate bridge with plastic explosive rather than keep chlorinated water out of your ears in the hotel swimming pool. (Note: If one of your ears is blown across the pool while swimming, you are using the wrong stuff.)

- Make sure all historical artefacts purchased have 'Made in Korea' stamped on the bottom. (Or, if you are serious about acquiring such artefacts at a reasonable price, consider taking one trip to Korea and collecting the lot.)

10 Excessive *kathedraal, duomo,* or *abbaye* exposure

There is a definite likelihood that if you are touring, in Europe especially, you will at some stage suffer from an odd complaint known as abbey fatigue.

It is a form of mental blankness. You see an abbey. You walk in. Walk out. Can't remember a thing.

At this point you must ration yourself to one abbey, cathedral or monastery per day or your whole trip will become a blur of flying buttresses. Severe cases have been found cowering in crypts muttering, 'I can't. I can't do another cathedral.' But if you take two theme parks and have a good lie down recovery is swift.

11 Ticket confirmation

When you ring your airline, what you confirm is that you are capable of using a foreign telephone system. That's it. You haven't confirmed your seat. The only way to confirm your seat on an international flight is to sit on it. To do this you must arrive at the airport early and spend several hours desperately clinging to the tie of the seat allocation clerk. This usually works. And good luck!

12 Duty-free shopping

Duty-free shopping allows you to buy all those electrical gadgets, big-name perfumes and designer doodads that you couldn't possibly afford at home, at such reduced prices that, flushed with excitement, you are forced to fan yourself with a collection of credit cards. Then you indulge yourself in such a shopping frenzy that your legs can barely carry the weight of your hand luggage on to the plane. You hope.

Naturally you arrive home to discover the prices are still cheaper at your local Stupid Sam's Discount Store. The designer scarf you bought is now being given away free with the exclusive perfume (you also bought), and the little TV set you bought in Japan is totally useless because it doesn't work in Australia.

To add to the pain, your credit card bill has just arrived showing the unexpectedly poor exchange rate used in all calculations.

13 Wildlife

The chances of seeing a deer, raccoon, hedgehog or even a limping quail in the wild in the country of its origin are considerably reduced if, on the way to the forest habitat, you notice that every second shop in every quaint little village offers goods and apparel for the sporting hunter. The reason for this is, of course, that every deer, raccoon, hedgehog and limping quail knows if they were to raise their heads in the forest, they may lose them!

To see wildlife in such countries you must visit a game park or zoo. This is also a safety precaution. If you were to raise your head in the forest in a remote mountain zone where local menfolk walk around with shotguns over their shoulders or drive around with loaded gun racks on their cars, you could be in trouble. You may look, at a distance, remarkably like a moose. Besides, you would not want to place temptation in the sights of gun-toting locals as they often don't like tourists and may not be able to resist the urge to cull.

If you are staying in picturesque accommodation abutting a forest and you hear trampling sounds in the shrubbery, I advise you to retire behind brick walls. There is nothing more off-putting for the tourist than to be hit in the chest with stray buckshot while drinking chianti on a terrace in Tuscany. The tour group that had this experience found the ambience of the evening was quite destroyed when one of their party was shot. He was mildly wounded. But the ambience was destroyed nonetheless.

14 Bed and breakfast burnout

The thought of starting the day with a big bumper of a fry-up of an English breakfast appeals to many travellers, hence the popularity of bed and breakfast accommodation.

The enthusiasm for such a concept is mostly a cost thing. The argument is as follows: if you can swallow a breakfast dripping in enough fat to drown at least one hysterical dietitian, then you won't have to eat again. Ever. Or, perhaps, not until the end of the day. This will save money.

Forget the fact that the average English breakfast of fried eggs, fried bacon, fried sausages, fried tomatoes and toast drowned in melted butter has so much cholesterol you can almost hear your arteries closing, and so little fibre you can feel your digestive system closing down. This is holidays!

Forget that on a normal day you only eat a bite of toast for breakfast, if you're lucky, during the daily mad-rush out the door. This breakfast will weigh you down for the rest of the day as if you had just eaten three tonnes of mixed cement.

Even forget that fact that your jaw is likely to seize up as there is a hell of a lot of chewing involved with this sort of major scheme breakfast.

Forget all that and eat.

Your plan will work until about the fourth day. Then you get out of bed, look a fried egg in the eye, and nearly vomit. Your system is saying: 'Please. Please. Hold the fat. We can't take it any more. Signed your loving liver, pancreas and assorted intestines.'

This is Bed and Breakfast Burnout. It can only be cured by moving to self-catering style accommodation though probably you will have forgotten how to open a packet of Corn Flakes.

15 War zone

You do not need to have graduated from Edward De Bono's School of Fundamental Logic to realise that if you travel to a war zone there is a possibility that you will be shot down, shot up or shot at, taken hostage or cut off from outside supplies for an indefinite period with a suitcase of dirty laundry and only half a packet of Tic Tacs in your possession.

On the positive side, a war zone does offer a lot of street theatre. And the plane travelling to and from the sand-bagged airport is usually pretty empty. This means it is very easy to get up-grades. And, as friends found when returning to Australia from Europe during the Gulf War, there was so much room on the plane each of the passengers on that long trip home got a bed, not just a seat!

But I must remind you, if you are thinking of travelling to a war zone, that acquiring those extra frequent flier points will be redundant if, in fact, bits of you end up flying in different directions.

16 The lone traveller

The lone traveller faces several unique problems. For instance, there is no one to whom you can say, 'Look at the magnificent vista.' The lone traveller just stands there thinking magnificent lone thoughts.

There is no one to take your photograph except total strangers, and they always hold the camera as if it's a landmine about to explode in their face. This is reflected in the resulting photograph, which has often been snapped at such an odd angle it looks as though it has been taken by someone suffering a heart attack.

There is no one to guard your luggage while you shop. It's a case of staggering around the airport shops knocking little souvenir ornaments off souvenir shelves, and of sitting with your luggage in the toilet.

In a foreign country, you have no one to converse with in your native tongue; you must smile a lot at locals in a dumb and hopeless manner. But if you overdo the smiling you soon find yourself surrounded by less-than-reputable local companions, and must fight vigorously to keep your aloneness and personal possessions intact.

There are, in short, many disadvantages associated with being a lone traveller. But you are the boss of your tour itinerary, the master of your travel destiny. And that counts. For, lone travellers take heed, travelling with a group can be worse. Much worse.

17 Group travel

Six or more companions tripping around together do not form a compact touring group, they form a mound of luggage that takes about three days to shift.

But luggage is the least of their problems. Travelling with a group, even of nearest and dearest friends, can be a nightmare starting with the fight to the verbal death on the grand issue of when to eat on the first night. The issue of 'Where to eat?' could take days to resolve, but is usually reduced to the limited tastes of the loudest whinger. 'I don't like Thai food.' 'But, for God's sake Margaret, you're in Thailand.' 'Can't we have Italian? Thai food gives me heartburn.' After a ten-minute historical tour with commentary down Margaret's digestive track, the decision is made: Italian food (with a slightly Thai bent as every host country has its own impact on imported cuisine).

And so it goes. Distances travelled are dictated by the health of the weakest bladder. Sights seen are determined by the least interested traveller. 'Haven't we seen enough temples? I want to go to the Casino.' Shopping times are reckoned by the most sluggish or committed shopper. Food eaten is dictated by the weakest stomach. Wine drunk is determined by the most stingy drinker. Distances walked are prescribed by the most stupid footwear. 'How could Cherylene bring high heels to the jungle?' Even adventures depend on the tastes of the least adventurous group member. 'I don't want to ride on an elephant. They wobble all over the place. Can't we take the bus?'

The problem of travelling with a group of six or more is that the whole production can quickly turn into a See-Nothing-Do-Nothing safari or a Bored-And-Bland tour. Alternatively, there may be a verbal punch-up on the third day where everyone airs their grievances or, more accurately, shoves their grievances down each others' throats, then everyone stomps off in different directions and enjoys themselves.

18 Travel companions, choice thereof

Having established that six or more travelling companions form a small, camera-toting insurrection, one can only conclude, to be on the safe side, that having one or maybe two travelling companions is close to ideal.

But there are certain prerequisites required of the ideal travelling companion which must not be overlooked.

The ideal travelling companion must be able to do their own laundry, carry their own luggage and look on the funny side of getting dysentery, or lost.

The ideal travelling companion must be cheerful or, at least, cheerful enough to make polite conversation *en route* to your destination as opposed to grunting at every landmark like a depressed yeti. This person should be fit enough to climb to a scenic viewing point without requiring you to carry them down again, and adventurous or, at least, adventurous enough to climb off the bar stool to visit a sight of greater interest than the bar room toilets.

The ideal travelling companion must be willing to share costs and in so doing they must not share a bunch of grapes by counting them, share a loaf of bread by dealing out slices like cards or share a length of Rookworst by measuring it with a ruler first.

They must not complain unduly about the cost of the bus fare, the takeaway coffee, the sandwich for lunch, the tourist monorail ride or the unbelievable entrance cost of the current attraction, or you may find yourself buying a souvenir cutlass whatever the cost and running them through before the tour is out.

> The ideal travelling companion must not snore.

The ideal travelling companion must be willing to share the driving and refrain from making snide little sarcastic comments about your driving ability and general incompetence while you are at the wheel. This more or less rules out any possibility of a spouse being an ideal travelling companion.

The ideal travelling companion must not snore. Accommodation problems aside, your travelling companion may fall asleep bedside you on a bus and all passengers on that bus will look to you for a noise pollution solution. And, I can guarantee, that travelling companions are never happy if they are woken up because in desperation you have placed a pair of yesterday's socks into their mouth.

And, finally, the ideal travelling companion must not have visited the Taj Mahal. Let me explain. I was sightseeing with a dear and devoted friend in Pisa. I was standing dumbstruck by the enormity of the history, the exquisiteness of the craftsmanship and the sheer magnificence of the white marble duomo next to the leaning tower. My dear and devoted friend's first comment was, 'You should see the Taj Mahal. There are metres of inlaid marble — just like this, but better.' I walked away. She followed. 'And the Taj Mahal has real gemstones embedded in the marble.' I walked away. She followed.

An hour later, while eating a gelati, my dear and devoted friend was still saying, 'And in the Taj Mahal they have ...' I cut her off mid-sentence. I wanted to say, 'If you mention the bloody Taj Mahal again I'll shove that gelati up your nose.' But I didn't. I just hissed, 'Stop talking about the Taj Mahal. We're in Pisa.' My ever-so-dear and slightly-less-devoted friend looked ever-so-slightly hurt. But it shut her up.

19 Visas

Visas are required in many countries to prevent some smart little officious upstart of a uniform-wearing public servant looking at your passport and shaking his head. This shaking of the head means you cannot come into this country and would you hurry up and leave as I want to have lunch. There goes the prepaid package tour. The fun in the sun. The undersized souvenir T-shirt and the oversized souvenir straw hat. The romantic stroll in the moonlight. This visa business is serious. It can affect your sex life. And the great visa fiasco has befallen you and torn half your holiday to shreds because this bloke-at-work's brother's girlfriend said you didn't need a visa. There's a line of authority you may never access again. After you kill her, metaphorically speaking, of course.

All you get out of this visa affair is a three-day wait — if you're lucky — sleeping in the airport transit lounge while some local official sorts out the details. Or maybe you score a three-day wait in the transit lounge while some local official fails to sort out the details and you are required to take the next plane — due in forty-eight hours — home. You are forced to ponder, as you return home with holiday snapshots of the interesting flushing mechanism of the local airport toilets that there never is a smart little officious upstart of a uniform-wearing public servant kicking around when you actually need one.

Perhaps, fortuitously, you do the right thing. Line up at the nearest consulate or embassy. Fill in the forms. Provide a photo. Wait. Read the texts explaining the population density and coastal drainage system of your destination. Wait. Look at the ricepaper prints on the wall. Admire the ashtray on the coffee table. Look at the other people waiting for visas. Decide they are all boring. Wait. Inspect your cuticles. Think about taking up smoking. Start inspecting the worn areas in the carpet. Rethink the global impact of the European Union trade policies.

Eventually you fork out some money for the relevant visa. The more money you pay, the better the stamp. That should make you feel good. Some countries even have upmarket holographic images on stickers. They make you want to forget the trip to stay at home and start collecting stickers.

So everything is in order but when you arrive in the relevant country no one looks at your face, let alone your passport. And you feel cheated. Conned. Ripped off. You have paid good money for this stamp, someone has to look at it. But they don't. And you have the honour of carrying around in your passport a fifty dollar sticker.

20 Lost passport and/or plane ticket

You will assume that if you are in a strange land and manage to lose your passport and plane ticket that you are in big trouble. Bigger than big trouble. We are talking trouble twice the size of Texas and double Ben Hur. And the loss of your passport and ticket will cost you dearly in terms of time, money, inconvenience, nervous energy, foot-stamping, and R-rated swear-word frustration. You will need a lot of swear words to cover this situation and you are bound to run out of profane expletives within the first fifteen minutes of discovering your loss.

On the other hand, nothing much may happen at all. Recently, a friend travelled from Rome to Melbourne without a ticket or passport, though she was travelling with an irritable, aggrieved and huffing husband.

The husband was a little irritable because he had managed on their last night in Italy to fall naked down some very solid stone steps in their idyllic villa. This left him suffering a shonky shoulder, stiff leg, and various degrees of indignity.

He was also a little aggrieved because his wife had purchased some souvenirs of their Italian experience, two folkart serving platters, which he pointed out 'weigh a bloody tonne' and 'are both the size of an average birdbath'. And, he felt obliged to add, 'How do you expect to get them home on the plane?' 'I'll carry them,' she replied. Marital harmony was held in balance by a mere thread of silent mutual disgust. Then it snapped. At the airport.

'What do you mean you can't find your ticket?'

'What! You've lost your passport too. I don't believe it. I don't bloody believe it. You didn't forget the souvenir plates. The ten-tonne of souvenir plates. Oh, no. You're walking around holding them in your arms as if you've given birth to them. But you leave your passport at the villa. And your ticket.'

He was about to make a rude comment on the state of mind of menopausal women. But he had second thoughts. That's the thing about menopausal women. They don't suffer contempt gladly. He could have ended up with two birdbaths smashed on his head.

They made enquires. Travelling without a ticket. No problem. Fill in this form. Travelling without a passport. No problem. Fill in this other form. And these friends made it home on time with little extra expense and only several patches of unresolved anger as their only inconvenience.

And all was well until several days later when the husband limped into the bedroom to hear his wife exclaim, 'Guess what? I've just found my passport and ticket. They were in this little zip-up section of my bag. I mustn't have looked there.' Finally all those patches of unresolved anger knitted together and exploded into the open, demanding attention.

I can happily say the marriage survived. The husband has regained full use of his leg and shoulder. And the folkart serving platters are an ongoing feature of dinner party conversation.

21 A room with a view

When you arrive at your pre-booked accommodation and are told that you have been given 'a room with a view, Monsignor', this may mean that the double doors in your hotel room open on to a vine-covered stone balcony where you can sit and sip a chilled white wine as you watch the azure blue waters lapping on to the sand of the secluded cove where local fishermen, from the nearby whitewashed village, sit contentedly singing as they mend their fishing nets.

Or a room with a view may mean that your twenty-five-storey hotel overlooks fifteen other high-rise hotels and the view you get from your room can be seen, on a sunny day, reflected in the tinted windows of the adjoining twin tower, or, on an overcast day, the view is provided by the same twin tower courtesy of those innocent tourists who don't realise they should pull the curtains.

Moreover, a room with a view is, by definition, a room with a window. And if that window is neither boarded up nor painted out, then what you see when you look out that window is the view even if it happens to be a panoramic vista of a brick wall, a stunning view of a multi-storey carpark, a breath-taking vision of a working sawmill or a grand vision of the knob on a flag pole on the top of Notre Dame.

I've seen them all. The first time I was in Paris I was told, 'Oui, Mademoiselle. You can see zee Notre Dame from zis room.' And you could. If you stood on the bidet in the bathroom and shoved your head out the tiny bathroom window without slipping and hanging yourself between the narrow sashes, then you could indeed see the top of one flag pole of Notre Dame. The sawmill was in Ireland. The brick wall was in Amsterdam.

22 Souvenirs

The problem with souvenirs is this: you buy them at a souvenir shop. And souvenir shops are often crammed with souvenirs that are so tasteless, so cheap, so irrelevant that a hat adorned with a full replica set of bagpipes seems like a good idea at the time. As does the Eiffel Tower toilet brush set, the Big Ben digital alarm clock, the Empire State Building/King Kong salt and pepper shakers and the Pantheon coffee table.

Souvenirs Russia (with and without steroids)

This is impulse buying at the most basic level for it links the reptilian part of your brain, which still thinks an iguana is an object of beauty, directly to the hand holding the credit card. A brain operating at this level naturally thinks that a musical, revolving, plastic gondola with moving gondolier is an *objet d'art* of irresistible charm and just right for the mantelpiece at home.

You just have to get out that exit and think about it for a few minutes and not only will sanity prevail, you won't do in your back trying to lug a damn awkward coffee table with Corinthian columns through customs.

23 Weather

There are two sorts of weather. There is tourist-friendly weather when the sun is shining, but not enough to cause contrast havoc with the instamatic. The birds are singing, but not attacking you at lunch. And the flowers are blooming, but not billowing rolling clouds of allergy-loaded pollen. Under these idyllic conditions tourists do not simply arrive at popular tourist spots, they swarm.

It might take you three hours to go up the Statue of Liberty but you only make it to her bosom because it's too hot in there. There may be a two-hour wait to get your foot in the lift of the Empire State Building. Now you know why King Kong went up the outside of the building. You could age so much standing in line to see the Crown Jewels at The Tower of London, they should give you a complimentary walking frame on the way out.

Then there is the other sort of weather. The horror weather for tourists. Wind blows the tourist map out of your hand. Rain soaks into everything you are wearing including your wallet. You are paying with soggy cash or with credit cards with no signatures. Roads flood. Cars stall. The power blacks out. You don't know where you are, where you're going or how you're going to get there. But the good news is, you are alone. More or less.

If you happen to stumble upon the Empire State Building in the torrential rain, it's yours, baby. You've got King Kong to yourself. No other fool of a tourist is out in that weather. Of course, in the photographs from the top of the Empire State Building, New York will look like a wide-angle shot of the inside of a grey school sock, but you didn't have to queue!

24 The *autoroute*, motorway, *autobahn* or *straatweg*

When travelling anywhere in the world you will notice that all autoroutes, motorways, autobahns or straatwegs look the same. The same ramps. The same signs. The same dotted lines. You can travel across an entire country and, what with bulldozed cuttings and being caught between large trucks, all you see is *autoroute*.

I would say travelling through any country entirely on the *autoroute* system is pointless. It's like having sex with a eunuch. You miss the important bits!

25 House key

Of course you take a house key with you when you go on holidays. Any fool would. But after an adventure-packed, all-action, touring holiday you can never remember where you put that key. You are standing at your own front door with your two suitcases, three bottles of tequila, your Mexican hat, your flamenco guitar, your genuine Totonac poncho, clutching your genuine matador's spear-like *baberillas* and prized decorated skull, and you can't get in. Did you put your key in your wallet, coat pocket, backpack or camera case? You can't remember. You open every bag. Your less-than-fresh laundry has exploded all over your doorstep and you still can't find your key. You are about to be arrested trying to break into your own house.

This almost happened to me. I wasn't arrested. But as I watched HRH smash his way into our house, I was thinking beyond divorce. I was contemplating murder.

THREE
IS THIS AIR PSYCHOTIC

or Do All Pilots Think 'We're Goin' Down' Jokes Are Funny?

GETTING THERE, SORT OF

We're on our way to Europe. I find the hysteria of getting to the airport quite invigorating: the packing, cancelling the paper, farewelling the budgie, dragging a semi-comatose teenager out of bed, counselling his travel-wary sibling out of throwing up until she is genuinely moving (and not just watching an airline ad on telly), calming HRH, who has an atomic twenty-four-hour clock inside his head alerting him to the fact that we are two and a half minutes behind schedule, and screeching in Cruella de Ville style, 'Where are my sunglasses? Somebody must have seen them!'

But there is more drama in store. The next major outrage of the trip unfolds at the airline counter. We had restricted ourselves to, more or less, one and a half pair of underpants each so we could carry our luggage on to the plane. In fact, our luggage was so compact that unpacking meant peeling our socks apart. Unfortunately, our bags were too heavy according to Australian regulations for cabin luggage.

Apparently, a bag once fell out of an overhead locker hitting some poor, unsuspecting passenger and causing grievous bodily harm with a suit pack! Having made tests and finding the

Australian Standard Skull can take an impact of up to six kilograms the limit was set. I watched all our luggage wobble down the conveyor belt to the cargo hold. 'The travel sickness tablets,' I gasped. Miss I've-changed-my-mind-I-don't-wanna-go-on-a-dumb-aeroplane immediately sobbed, 'I'll throw up all the way to Hong Kong.' I had to run around the airport at manic mother speed to locate more tablets. We now have enough travel sickness medication to supply five armies.

Then we sit and wait. And wait. Twenty-five minutes after arriving at the airport, I'm so bored, a yawn is a welcome distraction and watching other people yawn sheer entertainment. It gives me time to reflect on the ridiculous extremes of the travel experience.

Travel seems to involve long periods of listless, mindless boredom wedged between sudden outbursts of heart-jolting terror. The mind-numbing boredom may be associated with that four-hour delay at Heathrow Airport, Hong Kong Airport or Narita Airport. How do you fill in four hours at an international terminal? There is only so much duty-free shopping you can do. And after only a few international trips all the duty-free shops begin to look the same. You almost suspect that the same Hermés scarf, Chanel perfume, Glenfiddich Scotch, Grisham novel and a variety of souvenir T-shirts have been following you around the world.

You could prop yourself up at the international bar and get drunk. But the danger is that you could get so drunk you miss your flight, and then you have to negotiate for an alternative flight in a foreign language, with a hangover. And no change of clothes (they didn't get drunk; they're on the flight home).

You could, like I do, get really stuck into the cups of tea. But waterlogged to the eyeballs, you realise that your distressed kidneys will make your trip home hell. You are in Hong Kong. You're heading back to Australia, and you have just managed to turn yourself into the fifth little piggy. It's an eleven-hour flight, and you are going to wee, wee, wee all the way home.

Too tired to read. Too niggled to sleep. Too bored to talk. Too uninterested to eat. Too dazed to think. You end up zombied-out, just sitting there in the terminal staring at the passing parade. It's a form of suspended animation where you are not frozen, but jellied. And there you sit until the announcement 'now boarding' jolts the survival instinct back to life so you can claw your way on board. This seems to happen to everyone in the transit lounge. You board the plane in a sweaty rush of humanity, when you could wait. As if two more minutes would matter.

Like paranoid lemmings on a package tour, we charge towards the boarding ramp entrance in a family group. As we secure overhead baggage and settle into our seats, I become philosophical once more about the odd nature of air travel. It's funny, I muse, how boredom and terror can work in tandem. If you are a reluctant flier, the hand of terror grips your heart as you board the plane, and it continues to squeeze all rational thought from your mind. Your fate is sealed within that aluminium canister with wings. But after some time, the humdrum ordinariness of a long international flight takes over. You've watched the safety talk. You've read the menu. There are only fluffy clouds outside and a dubbed Chinese adventure movie playing on the screen, and there are ten hours of flight remaining.

The initial terror settles into the brain-dead world of boredom where you think about your numb legs, the foot that's gone to sleep, the crick in your neck. On and on. For hours. Or until the warning chime gongs and the pilot announces, 'Please fasten your safety belt, ladies and gentlemen. We're expecting a bit of turbulence ahead.'

Suddenly, the adrenalin pump splutters into action. And you are entertained by the wild imaginings of your terror once more, which includes instant reruns of every air-disaster movie you have ever seen, with you playing one of the stereotypical parts.

I'd be the hysterical mother screaming in a frenzy of terror as the plane skids to a halt on the icy runway. A nearby Bruce-Willis-type hero slaps me into reality, so that I can take action and save myself and my children. And all of this disaster scenario is rushing through my mind in a Pavlovian response to a little red light flickering the words 'Fasten Seat Belt'.

These are the images, shaded with foreboding or touched with the vivid colours of triumph, of just getting there.

THE LOWDOWN ON FLYING HIGH

As you know, it was mostly my idea to take the family on this European odyssey. 'Children do not,' I insisted, 'grow up and thank God for the quality carpet in their parents' lounge-room. They need memories.' Unfortunately, the teenage Master of Grunge and the young and curious nine-year-old from the School of Loud Questioning had the stamina necessary to whinge their way across three continents. Even before we arrived at the airport I suspected the major memory the children were likely to have of the trip was their mother's demonic face spitting out the words, 'If you two don't stop, I swear I'll leave you in an orphanage in Bulgaria.' Just three days of constant travel with the family, could make the idea of sitting at home for six weeks staring at the quality carpet quite appealing.

> I prayed there would be omelette left after the flight attendant had worked her trolley past the other 347 passengers.

However, we finally boarded the plane. Suddenly, all of those torture-chamber memories of past flights flashed into my brain. Travelling economy class for what amounts to twenty-two hours — if the wind is in the right direction — of air travel time is like taking the cheap package tour to hell in a chartered vacuum cleaner.

The background swooshing noise is relentless. Listening to Hugh Grant stumble his way through *Sense and Sensibility* was like watching a video with my head shoved down a flushing toilet.

The food was terrifying in its diversity. We were handed a menu — at what was probably 3 a.m. on our body clocks — to choose from Omelette with Herbs, or Fun Kuen with Shanghai Pok Choy. The Kuen may have been fun on the way down, but less fun on the way back up. I prayed there would be omelette left after the flight attendant had worked her trolley past the other 347 passengers. Even then, mysterious food items appeared with the omelette. We sensibly adopted the policy of not eating anything we didn't recognise so that we didn't mistakenly eat the refresher towel for dessert.

Sitting in a tangle of arms and legs with a child slumped on me from either side, I tried to sleep, but found myself frozen in a position only found playing a game of Twister.

So I whiled the time away watching the plane computer. This

was a mistake. The up-to-date information on speed, altitude, position, and so on, is meant to reassure the reluctant passenger. It doesn't work. On the trip from Australia to Hong Kong I watched the altitude go up, go down, go up, up, down, down. I felt like storming the cockpit shouting, 'Call yourself a pilot! You can't even keep the damn thing level.' And the speeds were all over the place. Even when we landed the altitude kept changing. I thought we must have landed on a trampoline.

The trip from Hong Kong to Amsterdam was worse. In every glossy airline brochure a smooth, curved, red line marks the flight path from one country to the next. The computer tells a different story. This was a 13 hour 14 minute flight. When the plane took off from Hong Kong the computer showed quite clearly that it was flying in the opposite direction to Amsterdam. What sort of idiot was flying this plane? Eventually the plane turned lazily towards India. Then what did it do? It followed what can only be described as a yak track through the Himalayas.

Finally — as would be expected — the pilot found Amsterdam, and immediately turned back towards Hong Kong. Twenty-five minutes later we landed. Stiff and weary from travelling, I shuffled off the plane bent double like the Hunchback of Notre Dame carrying about five kilograms of excess luggage in the bags under my eyes. But I tell you one thing, if the Pope had been on our flight, when he bent to kiss the tarmac, I would have beaten him to it.

I'M HEAVING ON A JET PLANE

I would like to draw your attention to the unique nature of the airline sick bag. Aeroplanes, ironically, just can't help looking like aeroplanes. A 747 pops out of the factory looking like a standard issue 747, except for the occasional outburst of corporate fervour painted on the tail fin or, indeed, on the entire plane.

Despite all the variations on interior design, integrated colour schemes, divider panel art and corporate carpet concepts, you cannot help but be overwhelmed by a sense of extraordinary familiarity as you shuffle down the aisle of an aeroplane, do up the standard-issue seat belt and flick through the printed items in predictable gathered pocket on the seat in front.

But the sick bag stands alone as a mark of independent

corporate thought. The airline passenger can be faced with variations in concepts from the plain brown bag to an intricate presentation of artwork on fine origami paper, so presumably, one can entertain oneself making little paper cranes, while one is being violently ill.

Loosely grouping the sick bags I have come across and read about, it may surprise you to know that:

1 I am not the only sanity-challenged person in the world interested in sick-bag art.

2 I'm actually the least loony of the lot because I am merely interested in them — other people collect them.

I have come to the vital conclusion that there appear to be three distinct schools of sick-bag design.

The first school follows the Bloomsbury school of literature, as in a sick bag is a sick bag is a sick bag. The bag is plain, and labelled 'Bag. Air Sickness. Stock No. 3905-112-100-9182'. Of course, if one is flying on an international airline one may be faced with an emergency interpretation of the words, *Spuckbeutel*, *Luchtziektezak* or *Sac Vomitoires* — though the last name is, of course, decipherable for English speakers, and I'm just a little disappointed the bag isn't clearly labelled 'Le Vomit'.

The next school of sick-bag design involves presenting a bag with a handy application other than that of being sick in. Air Afrique has childbirth instructions printed on the sick bag. And if, indeed, you are suddenly called upon to help the passenger sitting next to you give birth on an Air Afrique flight, you may, in your anxiety, be thankful for the use of the bag while following the instructions on the back.

TWA have a gin rummy score card printed on the back of their sick bag. The problem being, of course, that if you are in need of the bag but sitting next to mad-keen gin rummy players, you may have to wrestle them to the floor to get your hands on your own sick bag and generally secure your right to vomit.

Australian airlines have turned their sick bags into photograph-development envelopes. What does it all mean? I think, as most holiday snaps make everyone back home utterly sick, the idea is you fly away on your holiday, return home with pre-formed vomit in a film-processing bag to give to your friends, thus cutting out the middleman.

The most extraordinary school of sick bag design involves the totally vague. No indication is given on the sick bag as to its purpose. In the first instance, this is surprising as airlines label everything: 'A. Window seat. C. Aisle Seat. Toilet. Engaged. Hot Tap. Cold Tap. Aftershave. Close Latch for Take-off and Landing. Emergency Exit. Do Not Fill Brake Reserves With Other Than Specified Fluid.'

I have to admit that this last label worries me. If the maintenance crew are so stupid that they might attempt to put the wrong brake fluid in an aeroplane, why are we assuming that they are smart enough to be able to read. In fact, filling in time reading all the labels in an aeroplane only encourages more interest in, if not need for, the sick bag.

As we have not yet come up with an international stick figure symbol for 'vomiting person', I have to assume that the item in front of me is indeed the sick bag and hope, in cases of emergency, that I don't find myself vomiting, by mistake, on to my neighbour's duty-free perfume purchase.

The next time you are in an aeroplane and see the words 'Sac pour mal de l'air', remember that when it comes to airflight what goes up must come down, and, tragically, sometimes vice versa.

CATCH 22 REVISITED or Everything You'd Like to Know About Air Travel But Have Been too Drunk to Ask

I have watched the safety instructions on many flights. And I'm not happy. Not one little bit. Oh! I know where the emergency exits are, I am well acquainted with how to do up my safety belt, and I am fully aware that in an emergency little yellow masks will fall down in front of my face so that my last living moments will be spent in masquerade looking like a jaundiced pig.

But I feel the really big questions of air travel have never been properly addressed. I don't blame the airlines. I don't blame individual flight attendants. In my experience, flight attendants have been more than willing to answer any safety questions. But, if you are a paranoid air traveller like myself, the problem is that by the time you are buckled into your seat, holding a wet facewasher in one hand and an orange juice in the other, while trying to decide whether to go with the hyperventilation attack or assume the foetal position, the on-board safety pep talk washes over you like an all-too-familiar advertisement for headache tablets. And even if you could remember what it was exactly that you wanted to know about air safety, you are at this point in time either too drunk or too terrified to ask.

For the benefit of all paranoid air passengers I will address once and for all time the big questions of air travel.

The first question that we of Club Paranoia feel too terrified, drugged out or drunk to ask is, 'How do those bloody huge jumbo jets stay in the air in the first place?' My faith in aerodynamics only extends to kites. I can understand how kites fly. I understand how paper planes sail through the air. I can even grasp the fundamentals of Frisbee flight.

But jumbo jets are different. They weigh four hundred tonnes. Then they fill jumbo jets with over three hundred people including an unknown number of tourists carrying all sorts of camera equipment, duty-free alcohol and souvenir rocks. They add a dozen toilets — and who has ever heard of a flying toilet? — chuck in crates of champagne and bread rolls that seem to have been mud bricks in a previous life, and then they expect the damn things to fly. Is this reasonable?

Of course it is not reasonable! Have no faith in aerodynamics my friend. If aerodynamics really worked, the Flying Nun would be operating a regular service to the Vatican by now. There is only one thing keeping those jumbo jets in the air. We paranoid passengers. We sit there willing the aeroplane to stay airborne. We use telekinesis. And until it is proven otherwise, we will continue to keep those jumbo jets flying through the power of positive thinking. It's an exhausting task, but I can tell you from experience that it works.

The next question that the paranoid passenger is too drunk or terrified to ask is the most obvious. 'What about a parachute?' Airlines are very diligent in providing every passenger with a lifejacket, instructions on how to manually inflate the jacket and the correct use of the whistle to attract attention. Not that I've ever put much faith in the whistle myself. Any group of people who are too preoccupied to notice an airliner crashing into their part of the ocean is hardly, I feel, about to take much notice of a whistle, no matter how enthusiastically it is blown.

Moreover, on every flight we passengers, paranoid or otherwise, are shown where to find our lifejackets and the location of the sea-survival rafts, even if the entire flight will take place across land from, say, Adelaide to Darwin, when the only hope of landing in water would be if the pilot managed to crash the plane into one of the larger backyard swimming pools.

Airlines have the concept of crashing into the ocean sorted out. Aeroplanes have been designed, it would seem, for the specific purpose of crashing into water. We have lifejackets. We have reflective lights. We have whistles. We have a plan. But what if the we crash on land? What then?

I'll tell you what! It's all in the safety brochure. If an aeroplane is about to slam at a zillion miles an hour into *terra firma*, just before the catastrophic event passengers will be urged to 'Brace. Brace. Brace'. That is it! You are in an aircraft about to hit the earth in an unscheduled nose dive and you are offered, by way of reassurance and safety advice, to employ 'the Brace'. Arms folded on knees. Head down. If you are lucky, you get a ten centimetre by twenty centimetre pillow to cushion the impact.

And I, for one, am not impressed. If the Brace was such a successful anti-impact strategy then we would have been employing the Brace in the car-crash situation for years. Forget lap-sash seat belts. Forget airbags. Forget roll bars. Ladies and gentlemen, we have the Brace. The Brace will save lives.

If the Brace is the top line in safety instructions for a crash-landing, the paranoid passenger will immediately think, 'Why can't I have a parachute? They are tormenting me.' This can be explained. Most aeroplanes fly too fast for a comfortable exit by parachute. As you leave the plane your top half would be saying goodbye to your bottom half. Besides, at that altitude you couldn't breathe anyway, so neither half would survive. (Don't dismiss the power of modern medicine. Surgeons might be able to sew your top half on to another passenger's bottom half, and you'd be as good as new, as long as they used same-sex halves.)

But paranoid passengers are not to be dismissed so easily. 'But,' they exclaim, 'somewhere between 30 000 feet and the crash-landing, we must pass the ideal parachuting height. Then I could jump out. Why can't I have a parachute?'

It could be done. There is only one glitch in this plan. How do you get 300-odd passengers off a plane in ten seconds? I know what would happen. It would be first-class passengers first. By the time we got to my row in economy class the plane would have crash-landed.

In other words, forget the parachutes. We have the Brace. The pillow. And the safety brochure. Now, assuming we have just survived the crash-landing the next big questions are: 'Where are the emergency exits?' and 'Why didn't I pay more attention to the safety instructions?'

These questions are unnecessary. In every movie you are ever likely to see of an airline crash, there appears no need for emergency exits as the aircraft is ripped in half on impact. The surviving passengers spend no time whatsoever undoing emergency exit doors. They simply scramble out through the gaping hole. Why aren't we told this in the safety pep talk?

> But somewhere between 30 000 feet and the crash-landing, we must pass the ideal parachuting height.

'First, look for the gaping hole. If there is no gaping hole you may have to use the emergency exits located at the front or middle of the aircraft. Survivors are also advised that, in the case of a crash-landing in a remote part of the Andes, rows 1–24 should be eaten first.'

I doubt if the last statement will ever be added to the safety instructions, but being a paranoid passenger it always struck me that first-class passengers would make the best dishes, as they have generally been marinated for a long time in quality wine.

So there is little comfort to be had for the paranoid passenger regarding the crash-landing. There is the Brace. The pillow. The brochure. And the quiet knowledge that in the case of a remote crash location the first-class passengers will make the best casseroles.

But I can confirm the worst fears of the paranoid passenger, for I have met a plucky passenger who has survived a crash-landing. It was an American airline, and the emergency landing was at Los Angeles Airport. There can be no doubt: reality delivers a more severe blow than the most colourful extremes of the imagination. Here is a blow-by-blow description of the emergency landing.

1. The wheels won't descend.
2. The pilot explains that the wheels on one side are stuck. To help them descend he intends to drop one thousand metres quickly in the hope that he jolts them out. The domestic equivalent would be someone belting the television set with the vacuum cleaner. It's a standard procedure. When technology fails, give it a good bang!
3. It doesn't work. Well, it does work in one sense. Everything that is loose in the cabin relocates itself in someone's face. And those passengers who ate and drank a lot for dinner are regretting every heaving minute of their rash choice.
4. The passengers are then told they are about to experience an emergency landing.
5. The first thing flight attendants do in the case of an emergency landing is run for the staff emergency procedure booklet. This immediately reassures the passengers that absolutely no one knows what is going on.
6. By following the instructions on pages 2–14, the flight attendants are able to tell passengers with some authority what they should do, namely, 'Brace. Brace. Brace'. However, 'Brace' as yelled in a hysterical American accent sounds to the Aussie ear as like 'Brrr-aise', and you might suspect you are being invited to a barbecue, or a 'cook out' as Americans call it.
7. The gas masks drop. This is reassuring, except for the fact that the passengers are actually in the brace position and therefore unable to enjoy a quick whiff of oxygen.
8. The plane lands — or bounces along the tarmac, using the wheel casement as a prop.
9. No one is killed though life expectancies may have been reduced by the traumatic experience.
10. Passengers are urged to leave quickly via emergency exits. Slides are in place. Passengers must remove shoes. This is a sensible move as any women in stiletto heels will kill the person they land on at the bottom of the slide. And these slides are two storeys high. Can you imagine what it is like taking a two-storey slide? You are right. Friction burns are

nothing. If you lose your balance you are lucky to come out with your face in place.

11 You exit via slide. Then what happens is that three hundred people land on top of you. Arms are broken, ribs crushed. And this is a successful emergency landing.

12 The emergency crew do not know what to do with you. They are geared for casualties. They want bodies. They want bits of bodies. Their clipboards can't even fit all the names of the survivors. They don't know what to do with all of these people. They need to ask half the survivors to lie down and pretend they are dead. Then the emergency system could swing fluidly into action.

13 Passengers find themselves standing barefoot on the tarmac waiting for someone to decide what to do with them. I mean, after all, you would expect a few of the passengers to have the decency not to survive to give the emergency services something to do. Paramedics looked a little disappointed. It was a waste of good body bags. Really. No group was geared for this many survivors. 'Freaking hell' as American super-heroes are want to say. They all lived.

14 Passengers spend the next nine hours barefoot in transit. They have no passports. They have no money. Passports and money are still on the aeroplane. And nobody is going on to the aeroplane because it has just crash-landed. And nobody cares except the customs officers, who explain that you cannot enter the country without a passport.

15 Eventually passengers, passports and shoes are reunited. Life goes on. And paranoid passengers realise that between them and total chaos lies but a thin sheath of aluminium. And not much else.

THE RENT-A-CAR WAS FINE, I'm Returning My Husband!

Despite all this fear-of-flying hysteria, despite a severe case of bum fatigue (it has been sat on for over twenty-four hours with little relief), despite being in the company of two offspring with a wild children-of-the-damned look about their eyes, and despite the friendly companionship of an unbearably cheerful spouse, who — I believe — could do with a dose of sedation with a rubber mallet, we always miraculously arrive in one piece.

But before leaving any airport, we often must face one of the great traumas of the travel experience — aquiring a hire car. Together. Except for, perhaps, being trapped together for the winter in an Inuit igloo, hiring a car together is the ultimate test of a relationship. The test results in this case would, if written up in women's magazine style, read, 'You're on shaky ground.'

He likes to drive. It's a boy thing, so I let him. Unfortunately, I have inherited absolutely no sense of direction whatsoever. The north-south-east-west chromosome seems to have passed me by completely, and as a consequence I can get lost in an unfamiliar shower cubicle, and subsequently undergo a severe panic attack when I try to exit the cubicle through a brick wall.

Putting someone with the sense of direction of a dying blowfly in charge of the hire car while hurtling down, say, a French *autoroute* at 120 kph at night is like playing Russian roulette with six bullets.

> Opposites attract, they say. It worries me because I know I am a rational person.

'Turn left,' says HRH (His Royal Pig-headedness — it is a trait that emerges from his dark side whenever he takes hold of the steering wheel of a car. Naturally when I'm driving, he's even worse). 'Which left do you mean?' I ask. 'Left bloody left,' he replies. 'You don't have to get uppity about it,' I huff. Then I turn right, cut off a thundering four-tonne Mercedes Guterwagen and miss our turn-off by one hundred kilometres. A natural mistake I would have thought. But he gets very upset about it.

So he drives. This should solve all problems. It doesn't. Opposites attract, they say. It worries me because I know I am a rational person. And there have been times when he's driving on the scenic route through the Tuscan Alps with one hand on the wheel and his head under the dashboard that I realise I've married a homicidal maniac. And I can tell you something about

IS THIS AIR PSYCHOTIC? 95

homicidal maniacs. They don't like being told how to drive a car. Of course, this does not stop me offering sound advice or, where appropriate gasping, snorting, screaming or having a heart attack. As a consequence I have been told, in no uncertain terms, to stop breathing for the rest of the trip.

We have many disagreements about the appropriate approach to driving a hire car. I believe, for instance, you should get into the hire car, grip the steering wheel firmly with both hands and drive steadily off. He believes you should jump into the hire car, head down the nearest *autobahn* or *autostrade* and then, even though you are driving at night in the rain on the opposite side of the road, try out all the knobs and buttons on the hire car. 'Oh, look. It's a cigarette lighter. Oh, what's this? It must be the air conditioning. That must be an FM radio station. Look. That's how you open the boot.' In the meantime, I am watching the road gasping, 'Look! Look! That's a lorry approaching.'

Having argued our way through every knob and button and opened every window and door, we then proceed to the next major conflict of the hire car experience: reading the map. 'I'll read the map,' I insist. 'But you don't pay attention,' he protests grabbing it out of my hand. 'Well give me a chance,' I gasp grabbing the map back. And ripping it, which for some reason puts him in homicidal-maniac-plus mode. But he's right. I don't pay attention. For good reasons.

Either I have exactly two and a half seconds to make up my mind and give my beloved clear and direct instructions as to which turn-off we have to take as we hurtle at 80 kph around a foreign roundabout in peak hour. And, frankly, I need more time than that so we must hurtle around the roundabout at 80 kph at least twice, if not three times, by which stage HRH has that look on his face that suggests he could have played the active part in the shower scene from *Psycho*.

Or we are cruising through the English, Italian or perhaps French countryside and I am expected to pay full and complete attention to road signs and nothing else but road signs. I don't. I'm looking, not surprisingly, at the scenery.

'What did that sign say?' he demands.

'Dunno,' I reply. 'I was looking at that old castle over there. Isn't it fantastic?'

'You are meant to be the navigator.'

'What is the point,' I retort, 'of going on a motoring trip if you don't see anything but road signs?'

His usual reply is, 'Mutter, mutter, mumble ... What did that road sign say?'

'Okay. I got that one. It says 'Sortie'. Hold on. I'll look it up in the phrase book. It means ... wait a minute ... Exit.'

'I don't want the exit. I want to know if we're on the right road to Liege.'

'How should I know?' I sniff.

'You would if you were paying attention.' This is like *déjà vu* from hell. And it can go on for up to 250 kilometres.

But our biggest battle in the hire car involves the rattle.

It's another bloke thing. Sensible, mild-mannered men change, in a flash, into wild-eyed monsters of the motorways, and there is only one reason why this happens. And one reason alone. Their car, their beloved chariot, their phallic symbol on wheels has developed one of the most diabolical problems of the hi-tech motoring world. A rattle. And every hire car we have ever hired has a rattle.

His eyes bulge. He starts to twitch and foul utterings pour out of his mouth. For somewhere in the car, there is a rattle (whirr, clatter or hum), and according to HRH, life, including Western civilisation as we know it, will never be the same again.

It will certainly never be the same again for any member of the family who happens to be a passenger in the car with Mr I-Can-Hear-A-Rattle.

'Sssh!! Turn that stereo off. Stop breathing. I can hear a rattle,' he rants. And the great hunt for the rattle begins.

'Take everything out of the glove box. No. I can still hear it. Put everything back in the glove box. Put your left hand on the glove box lid. Put your other hand on the seat belt buckle. Put your right foot on the ashtray. And your left knee on the heating vent.' This is a great game for the passengers. It's called peak-hour Twister. The more players the better.

'Would someone put their hand on ashtray in the back? And someone else put their foot on the rear speaker. That's better.' Naturally, Mr I-Can-Hear-A-Rattle would expect the family to go for a two thousand kilometre drive twisted in knots, so he doesn't have to listen to a rattle. But the game of Twister rarely solves the problem.

'No. I can still hear it. Take everything out of the glove box again. Now put your head in and listen.'

Passengers offer some resistance to this suggestion especially females of the wife variety.

'I am not putting my head in the glove box. You're driving like a maniac who could easily crash the car. I'm not dying with my head in the glove box.'

'Just do it.'

Resistance is useless.

Now there are two possibilities here. Either the rattle stops. Or it doesn't stop. If the rattle stops I have a problem.

'That's it. It's stopped.'

'Good,' says I, taking my head out of the glove box.

'No. It's started again. Put your head back.'

'What are you trying to say? It's my head that's causing the rattle? What do you think? I've got a loose bolt at the neck?'

'Put your head back. See it has stopped.'

As I, the once Mrs Mild-Mannered-Tourist and now the hissing, scathing Mrs Divorce-Is-My-Middle-Name take my head out of the glove box, a bolt of revelation hits my beloved. 'You're wearing those rattling earrings again. AREN'T YOU?' I take them off. A strained silence descends on the touring family group.

Alternatively, the head in the glove box may not do the trick. The rattle lives on. This calls for drastic action.

'You drive,' he snarls. 'And I'll find it.' This signals the onset of many bizarre behaviours including checking under the dash, the children's teeth and asking if any of us are wearing faulty pacemakers.

His search will continue until we take the hire car back. That's why I'm tempted to say: 'The hire car was fine. I'm returning my husband. The problem is a rattle. I think it's in his head!'

FOUR
EUROPE
The Pink, Green and Yellow Bits

Europe fascinates me! So much tortured history, ancient culture and daily drama are squeezed into the complex mosaic that is Europe. The pink bits, the green bits, the yellow bits are all startlingly different yet separated by only a dotted line on the map.

And these fragments of the mosaic, often so tiny they represent no more than a thumbprint on the map of Australia, have rich histories that stretch back in the time to when the great south land drifted away from mother Europe and slipped down into the Southern Hemisphere.

Visiting Europe for an Australian is also, in part, a journey to the birthplace of our suburban homeland. For sprinkled across Australia, mainly in the cities, are slices of Italy, fragments of Greece, little bits of Germany, patches of Spain, a touch of Holland, a dollop of Scotland, great chunks of Ireland, and everywhere from our education system, to our form of government, to our inherited legal system, to the structure of our public service, to our insane love of tea and cricket, there lies the profound influence of the British.

Often in Europe an Australian can be haunted by the familiar ghosts of *déjà vu*. To be served a cappuccino by an Italian, a souvlaki by a Greek, to partake of a cream tea in Devon, shortbreads in Edinburgh, or to down a pint in a pub in Ireland is, for an Australian, nothing to write home about — such experiences are a daily occurrence in Australia.

On the other hand, to see a culture, a people *en masse*, is to appreciate an entirely new dimension of eccentricity.
- Italian drivers are the living proof that the chaos theory works.
- The Germans make food much the same way as they build cars. Solid. Dependable. And easily converted to natural gas.
- The English have turned queuing into a national sport. Unlike the rabble-rousing republicans over the channel who stormed the Bastille, you gain the definite impression that the English would queue in a riot.
- The Swiss are an efficient people obviously obsessed with time/motion studies as they have given the world muesli and cuckoo clocks.

Europe calls to me always. I want to lose myself in all this eccentricity. Again and again. In the meantime, here are tales of some of the colourful bits.

THE NETHERLANDS: Clogs, Sex and Bicycles
Amsterdam: canal and carnal capital of the world

Our first trip to Europe with the entire family troupe begins in Amsterdam. There is me, HRH, the teenage Master of Vague, and Ms Junior Stormtrooper. HRH, His Royal Hopefulness, is hopeful, in the beginning at least, that the itinerary he has planned down to three-minute intervals will be adhered to by the rest of the family. Ha! Ha!

We arrive at Schipol Airport hardly suffering the effects of jet lag. But jet lag is, of course, like a hangover on time delay. You bound around in the morning then, at about two in the afternoon, your face starts to lose its grip on your skull and droops, and your brain suddenly loses its grip on the third dimension leaving you drinking coffee by pouring it down your shirt front.

The vast, echoing and terrifyingly clean corridors of Schipol Airport live up to my most highly polished dreams of Amsterdam. Alas, my dreams are short-lived as we stumble out of customs into the finest examples of Dutch youth heading to a Eurocup soccer match, wearing metre-high red and white top-hats and matching scarves, and blowing plastic trumpets, playing tom tom drums and swilling beer at eight in the morning.

On a personal level, my arrival in Amsterdam is spectacular. We are meeting members of our long-lost family in Amsterdam. So excited am I by the moment, I stand backwards on the moving pavement without — how shall I put this — allowing for an elegant disembarkment. I am catapulted off the moving pavement on to my backpack which, weighing around ten kilograms, leaves me spinning on my back doing an instant impersonation of a dying blowfly in the middle of Schipol Airport. At this stage, my immediate family disown me, hoping, I suspect, that the Netherlands *ploitie* will drag me off for drug rehabilitation or hit me with an oversized fly swat.

On recovering my dignity, the family reclaim me, and we are met by our long-lost relatives in a Honda Civic. By various modes of transport we all head for the heart of the city.

Amsterdam would have to be one of the most magical cities on the face of this cold and logical earth. A city interwoven with a network of canals, narrow cobbled streets and quaint stone bridges, Amsterdam's old-world character is dictated by its buildings. Row upon row of red-brick houses with ornate curved facades are finished with white trimming which appears to have been piped on from an icing bag.

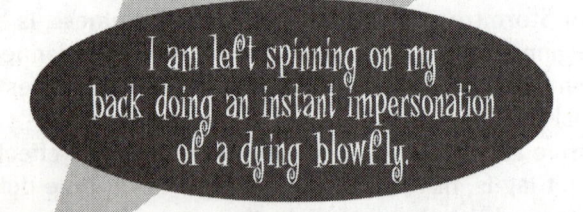

> I am left spinning on my back doing an instant impersonation of a dying blowfly.

As for the people, the first thing you notice about the Dutch is the language. I rather suspect the Welsh and the Dutch conspired to confound the English by inventing words of such length that an Englishman would need a pith helmet and compass just to locate the middle syllable. Not only are foreigners forced to stumble over words such as *sthoteldoekje* (dishcloth) and *sietsventieldopje* (bike valve cap) — I write these words down in my *notitieboekje* (note book) — these words seem to be pronounced by stopping mid way to swallow your tongue!

The Dutch, however, exhibit a unique matter-of-fact attitude towards two profound subjects, which seem to intimidate other cultures, namely bicycles and sex. I cannot over-emphasise the pragmatic nature of the Dutch. They are not upset by people taking drugs, but GODVERDOMME, they don't want untidy collections of junkies cluttering public places. So they put blue lights in railway stations and public toilets so junkies can't see their veins. The Netherlands may be the only country in the world where junkies break into houses to use the bedside lamps.

Amsterdamers also have to face the prospect that the only available space to park their cars is in their own living room. No one thought to include garages in the charming 17th-century houses. Parking a car in Amsterdam therefore involves about the same cost and inconvenience as landing a golf cart on Mars. If you find a car parking space in Amsterdam you not only fall to your knees offering thanks to Carportia — the Goddess of Empty Car Spaces — you also cough up around $A35 a day for the privilege, which is more than we would want to pay for the rent of a car.

To keep a car in Amsterdam, the Burgemeester and fellow burgers came up with a scheme whereby you must own a car for two years before you can obtain a licence to park it in the street. Work that one out. Where do you keep your car for those two years? In the freezer?

As a consequence Amsterdamers of all ages, sizes and athletic ability, ride bicycles. It is not unusual to see punk-rockers, omas and opas, businessmen in suits with briefcases and mobile phones, and even mothers with shopping bags, baby and pusher, all wobbling past on bicycles. But not swish bicycles. Here in the land where, if Shakespeare were to put pen to paper, Richard III would have swapped his kingdom for a bicycle, the bicycles are old rusted rattletraps without gears, metallic duco or even hi-tech hand grips. Amsterdam is, it seems, the graveyard for bicycles. Bicycles come from all over Europe to die in Amsterdam.

Amsterdamers peddle rust-buckets for one reason. Theft. In fact, you are lucky in Amsterdam if your bike is stolen after you get off it rather than before. 'You must budget for, at least, two bikes a year,' explain our long-lost relatives while not suggesting this involves a great outlay of gilders. Nevertheless, if an

Amsterdamer loses their bike, real pain is suffered in the face of a great loss. They grieve for the lock, which may have had the latest in locking technology, tungsten alloys and digital programming. In fact, Lock Loss Therapy is probably just around corner in Amsterdam.

Sex is another matter. Pragmatic as ever, the Dutch attitude to bonking in all bonk forms is: 'Everyone has sex, what's the fuss?' You can pick up a family magazine in Holland and find recipes, a knitting pattern, kinky leather fetishes and gardening advice. The posters gracing every lamp-post near our hotel in Keizersgracht show a naked man and a naked woman standing together, doing something only possible for consenting adults, with her in rollerblades and him wearing high-heel boots. I don't know what position this is called, but it looks downright dangerous.

Because we are travelling with our young graduate of the School of Loud Questioning, I am constantly put on the spot. In the end, I explain this particular poster to her, and the other 395 known positions displayed in postcards and souvenir tea towels with the words, 'People do funny things in Amsterdam. It's an allergic reaction to tulips!'

It's almost true. Our long-lost relatives fall off their chairs laughing when I tell them we wear bathing costumes in many saunas in Australia. I daresay if they could have got their hands on a poster of 'Saunas Downunder' they would have plastered the photographs all over Amsterdam to demonstrate the strange-but-true sexual practices of those wacky Australians.

The family spend a fair amount of time in Amsterdam 'nude spotting'. Postcards cover most of the known positions of copulation on rollerblades along with playful photographs of decorated reproductive anatomy of both sexes — the highlight being, I feel, the male genitalia decked out to look like Groucho Marx!

We find shops with marzipan nudes in deckchairs, and grinning penis salt-and-pepper shakers. We stumble into the redlight district at 5 p.m to see assorted naked women in windows — an indecently early hour, if you ask me. I don't think it's right for a girl to don ostrich feather scuffs, false eyelashes and feather boa one minute before 9 p.m. when the light is — I shall try to be delicate here — working in her favour! After all this, I decide Amsterdam is a dangerous city. A very dangerous city, indeed. Once distracted, and there are many distractions for the novice tourist in Amsterdam, one could inadvertently step in front of a speeding cyclist and end up with novel rearrangements of one's reproductive anatomy in a bicycle wheel. On the other hand, you might make some money from the photographs!

Children of the global village
I cannot tell you this story without relating a little of our family history. Believe me, you wouldn't want any more.

HRH has two children by a previous marriage and a granddaughter. He was, he insists, a child bride. So one aim of this major family pilgrimage to Europe is to allow our children to meet their brother and sister and niece. Being a family of the modern era, however, generation lines have blurred so much that our daughter, who is nine at the time, is meeting her seven-year-old niece. And there we all sit in a hotel room in Amsterdam one fine spring afternoon being overly friendly and awkwardly self-conscious.

We have to do something. Just sitting there in a cramped hotel room smiling at each other all the time is starting to strain our face muscles. So we decide to visit the Rijks Museum. It isn't far. We can walk.

Another factor adding to the discomfort of the moment is that our children — the aunty and uncle — can only speak English and their niece can only speak Dutch.

But the social ice is soon broken, shattered into little pieces all over the floor of the Rijks Museum. For, standing in front of the solemn glory of Rembrandt's *The Night Watch*, the nine-year-old Aussie aunty and the seven-year-old Dutch niece, find one word in common.

'Shit.'

And all the parents act with the same immediate response hissing, 'Shhhhhhh!'. To no avail.

One of the impish girls stands in front of yet another Rembrandt, points to it and says 'Shit.' And the other roars laughing, with the parents trailing after them both like deflating tyres hissing, 'Shhhhh!'

Once the *sh*-with-an-*it*-word hits the communication fan all social awkwardness vanishes in the uproar.

And that's the absurd memory we have of the Rijks Museum. If you ask my kids, they'll tell you it's a heap of. You know.

We have ways of making you walk
In the way of making memories, the children will never forget those foreign words their parents utter in Amsterdam. 'Walk. Yes. You have to walk. We haven't got a car. It's not that difficult; all you have to do is put one foot in front of the other. Remember?' For one terrifying moment I think I will have to drag my children by the ankles through the cobbled *straats* of Amsterdam. But I find by dangling the prospect of a CD in front of one and of lollies in front of the other, they slowly grasp the concept. We walk all over Amsterdam at the reasonable rate of only twenty-five moans per city block.

High culture meets the low-down video game
I had ideas about the cultural value of this trip to Europe. 'No Game Boy,' I say. 'No computer games. Period. This is an educational tour.' I last twenty-four hours. We bought a Game Boy and a thirty-game pack in Hong Kong. It shut one of them up for some of the time. But the Game Boy produces its own shadow of conflict.

The nine-year-old, tragically, becomes permanently fixed in the head-down Game Boy playing position. In the Van Gogh Museum I explode, 'You, madam, are going to look at one Van Gogh if it kills me.' She does. She slowly stops playing the Game Boy. She looks up and snorts, 'Hmmph. I could do that.' If you saw some of Van Gogh's lesser haystacks, you'd probably agree.

FRANCE Long Live *Joie de Vivre!*
Oo-la-la Paris by car!
This is the tragic tale of two people, one car and the disintegration of a marriage. My marriage. That is not the complete truth. The marriage is still limping along, held together by sticky tape and chewing gum. But if we hire one more car together ... forget divorce ... one of us will end up on charges of assault and battery with a road map!

HRH argues, as usual, that I am not paying enough attention to reading road maps and road signs. While I argue that it is unfair to expect me to read a road sign that whips passed me in a blur at 130 kph, especially one written in French. My French isn't up to it. All I learnt at school was: *Le chapeau de ma tante est sur la tete*. (The hat of my aunt is on the head.) This is not exactly useful French. The French phrasebook we bring with us is not much better. When you need to ask: 'Where the hell is Bologne?' all you can scrape together from the phrasebook is: *Ma carpe est malade*. (My goldfish is sick.)

> The only road signs I can read with any clarity are tolls.

Besides, once I pick up the road map of France I make a tantalising discovery. 'My God,' I gasp. 'The map of France reads like a menu. Look. There's Camembert, Champagne, Bordeaux, (Quiche) Lorraine, Dijon and the river Brie.' Come to think of it, any French village sounds good enough to eat. I'd eat La Ferte-Bernard, even if it was ferret *flambé*.

The only road signs I can read with any clarity are tolls. The French autoroutes are as smooth as french mustard — expensive french mustard. After forking out $A30 in tolls, I feel as if I own a little bit of the *Autoroute de L'est*. These autoroutes are also quite terrifying. Where two meet, you are looking at a freeway system designed like a bowl of flat pasta. Take the wrong turn and you end up in Spain. Lose confidence and you'll be stuck driving in circles for the rest of your life.

HRH shouts, 'Which lane do I take?' I shout back, 'How should I know?' I can only say the God of Freeway Systems was looking after us as we end up on the A4 with no recollection of how we got there. The real trouble begins, however, at the end of the freeway system in the heart of Paris.

Paris in peak hour is a city overrun with a plague of wheeled pests. That's what it feels like. 'We need DES CHAMPS ELYSEES,' HRH snorts. 'This is the AXE ROUGE,' I reply with authority, adding 'This road is the AXE ROUGE too. And this one.' It is my French again. The street sign I am so dutifully reading is 'No Parking (Red Area).'

We find DES CHAMPS ELYSEES as we either had the choice of going insane, going into the Seine or running into DES CHAMPS ELYSEES and, horror of horrors, that's when we find ourselves heading towards the world's most terrifying roundabout: the ARC DE TRIOMPHE. It should be renamed the ARC DE SUICIDE. Motorists, ten abreast, whiz around the Arc de Triomphe with one foot on the accelerator and one foot on the car horn. It is like dodgem cars without dodging. You do not actually drive a car in Paris. You bluff your way through.

> You do not actually drive a car in Paris. You bluff your way through.

I am having a nervous breakdown and I am only back-seat driving. HRH manages to add to my nervous twitch by putting the car in gear saying, 'I think the best thing to do is not look.' After moving around the Arc De Triomphe in positions found only in high-speed chess, we come across one of the most beautiful sites I am to see in Paris. Hertz rent-a-car. We can give the car back. From then on, we walk or catch that wonder of the subterranean world, the Metro.

Being a pedestrian in Paris, however, is no easy matter. I can't get the hang of it. Cars drive though red lights, green lights, and at the gendarmes. The idea is, I think, when you come to a pedestrian crossing, you wait for a lull in traffic, you take one step forward and if your face isn't taken off by a passing truck, you run for your life.

Teaching your children to look right then left then run like bloody hell is one of many things a parent soon picks up along the way in France.

I can, in fact, offer some advice for parents contemplating taking their children to Paris. Firstly, do not promise telly in the hotel. There is television. The children watch 'Alf' in German, Australia's own 'Neighbours' dubbed in French, Bruce Willis talking Dutch and the BBC World News Service. But as the children showed no interest in the British 'White Paper on Education' or the Israeli elections, I was constantly given looks from sour-faced children which said, 'You will pay, Mother, for dragging us halfway around the world to this as good as TV-less den of torture.'

Secondly, if you are travelling with children I advise you not to stay in the Moulin Rouge district. The Moulin Rouge is the capital of sex shows and takeaway food outlets in Paris — I'd find myself at a corner having to choose between passing pictures of live sex on a motorbike, or McDonald's. What sort of choice is that for a parent?

And, of course, while looking for souvenirs the young and curious member of the family found an action-figure key ring with two naked men and a woman. 'What are they doing?' she asks (again!). 'I don't know,' I reply, ' I think it's one of those puzzles no one can work out.'

But what could be better in Paris than strolling down Rue La Fayette on a magnificent day in spring? I feel like bursting into song — just like a coffee commercial.

Everything about Paris is as elegant as every word an impoverished poet holed-up in an attic in Montmarte ever wrote. It is romantic. It is chic. But, then again, anything can sound romantic in soft French syllables. The first sign I come across in France is 'Merci de Payer A la Boutique', which means please pay at the ESSO shop. ESSO petrol station shops are no 'boutiques'.

But I am prepared to get lost in the romance of it all. My romantic delusions, however, do not last. The problem is tourists. They truck them in from Germany, bus them in from Holland and parachute them in by the Concorde load from the U S of A. It is the invasion of Normandy all over again except the Americans are sending in highly trained squads of polyester-clad retirees shooting video cams from the hip, and this time the Japanese join in.

At the top of the Eiffel Tower ($A18 for a ride in a lift packed with vertical sardines carrying cameras), there are glorious views of Paris, if you can get an unrestricted outlook without someone's elbow in your face.

I would have left France feeling that it is a French Territory recently captured by militant middle-aged tourists, but for one experience. On the way into France, we stop for dinner at a friend's house at Rombas, near Metz. We had sent greetings to each other by fax for some time. Roberte and Jean-Claude welcome us into their home with such enthusiasm, it is terrifying. How can we ever repay their hospitality?

We are served sweet canapes, savoury canapes, champagne, then an entrée (*Foie Gras D'Oie* — it's not pâté, it's 'une' delicacy) and special wine. Main course was *Magret de Canard* and special wine. (I couldn't read the wine label this time, but it did not say Cheap Plonk.)

Next, cheese — Rochford, Brie, Camembert — and special wine. Then Roberte croons, 'Now for dessert.' Images of *La Grand Boeuf* sweep through my brain. The French always eat cheese before dessert. Not realising this, I had left only a little corner behind my left ear for dessert. Wild berry tart with natural ice-cream and special wine. After dessert, a cake and champagne. It was death-by-cuisine. At 2 a.m. Jean-Claude takes us for an enthusiastic tour of Rombas.

I realised that the heart of a country cannot be found in its grand monuments or pompous politics, but in the spirit of its people. It was within a French home that I discovered the warm heart of France.

Monet, Monet, Monet — it's a rich man's world

Grief is a journey. And any trip undertaken because of a death, or during the grieving process, involves an extra struggle with a heavy emotional load.

And so it was for me on our trip to Monet's garden in Giverny, a good one hour out of Paris.

My mother had died the previous year and left me some money. Not in an orderly fashion. We found some share certificates in a shoebox, with old Christmas cards and a bicycle pump, in one of her overcrowded wardrobes. But this was typical of a mother who spent far more time in my childhood generating fun by chasing us kids around the backyard with buckets of water than inside doing housework.

She was the mother who, on finding me sobbing after school because I was too tired to do my Grade 3 writing homework, sat down and did it for me in painstakingly forged New Script. And I burst in the door the next day yelling, 'Mum, I won a holy picture for best handwriting!' And she congratulated me.

She was my licenced driver when I sat for my driver's licence, chatting non-stop — she was a natural anyway — to Peter Pierce the local constable so he wouldn't ask me any difficult questions or notice my mistakes. And it worked. He asked me only three questions. And one was: 'Steep Descent. Is that uphill or downhill?'

When Mum died I had a great need to fill that aching void in my heart. This was another emotional dimension to my mid-life crisis. I couldn't do anything sensible with the money. That would only add to the pain. And so it was that I convinced everyone in the family we should go to Europe.

In France, I am adamant that there is a holy pilgrimage we must honour. Our family must visit Monet's garden because my mother was potty about Monet. She had Monet calendars all over the place. She used Monet colours in her silkscreen painting. And, significantly, not long before her death, my mother had given my daughter a book called *Linnea in Monet's Garden*. It's the story of a little girl visiting the garden. Mum inscribed the book to her granddaughter with words that seem prophetic now: 'To remember moments we've shared with laughter and our creative spirits working together making endless toys forever.'

I had to go to Monet's garden. But planning a pilgrimage of the heart is like loading a gun with emotional shot which when fired in haste only adds another wound to the list. Possibly in the region of the foot. For nothing is as you want it to be and the trip to Monet's garden is no idle exception. However, the greatest treasure my mother left me was our shared sense of humour, and as we bumble our dedicated way to Giverny, my mother, I suspect, was watching our escapades from above, rolling around on her very own multi-coloured cloud hooting with laughter.

We start the trip by arriving at Gare du Nord with five minutes to spare before the train leaves. I have no working French and no sense of direction, but this doesn't stop me yelling, 'Quick. You get the tickets, darling. The kids can follow me to the platform.' Running with my nose in the air trying to spot platform numbers, I manage — with pathetic apologies — to knock one cripple completely off his crutches, terrify one baby by tripping over its pushchair, and stumble over an ashtray, filling one of my sandshoes with ash, to arrive five minutes late at the wrong platform (with me still shaking a leg to offload the ash).

The only other train to Vernon, the station nearest Giverny, leaves three hours later and arrives one hour after our guidebook says that Monet's garden closes. The family looks at me as if the only honourable way out is to throw myself under the next train to Rouen.

I say, 'We pay. We go.' We already have the tickets to Vernon. 'And we shall see Monet's garden by looking over the fence. With mirrors if we have to.' I am adamant.

Three hours later after making a quick dash around the Arc de Triomphe and feeling anything but triumphant we stand on the right platform at the designated time with a hoard of fellow pilgrims.

The train pulls into the station. There follows an instant stampede which leaves three members of our party choking on a rising bloom of dust on the platform. My family are innocents abroad all right, which translates into basic travelling terminology as 'tourists without a seat'.

Whereas, I, the parent, who (according to some) cannot be taken anywhere in the world without making a public spectacle of herself, secure a seat by adopting the storming-of-the-Bastille technique. I surge in with the masses, then lunge sideways out of the throng to secure a seat with a rugby try.

HRH (His Royal Haughtiness) believes life should be conducted at a level of dignity above wrestling strangers for a seat. He is struck with a typical gentlemanly outburst of sangfroid, and stands back and lets two hundred tourists thunder aboard ahead of him, leaving him — a man of Burl Ives 'Big Daddy' proportions — floundering like a groper trying to fit into an already-packed can of sardines.

Naturally, I keep him a seat. He squeezes through the crowd and falls into the seat beside me huffing with an autocratic air, 'There's no need to rush.' I make a mental note not to take him with me to the next revolution. If he'd been involved with the storming of the Bastille he would have arrived three days late and expected catering.

The children emerge from the scrum in need of oxygen. We find we can perch one ungrateful child on the end of our seat making room by breathing in for the entire trip. Meanwhile, the adolescent stands for the duration in preference to sitting on the two-centimetre band of seat left beside a nearby sleeping, snorting one-hundred-kilogram Camembert cheese of a Frenchman with the twenty-per-cent-proof alcohol breath.

We rhythmically clatter on to Vernon in the hot, airless, sweat-drenched and crowded second-class carriage with the grime-smeared windows which turn visions of the French countryside into Van Goghesque swirls of green and beige. And on we clatter. Hot and irritable. An outlook which is only exacerbated as the stomach of a standing passenger bounces off my head.

It is about mid-way through this rail journey-cum-modern form of tourist torture that I utter the traveller's standard motto, 'Never again.'

But, of course, there is an again. The return trip. Meanwhile, we know we have arrived at Vernon because all the sardines start jumping out of the can. We disembark, resume normal breathing patterns and board a bus.

After a fifteen-minute ride in an old swaying war-vintage bus, we arrive at Monet's garden. It is open after all. And it is glorious.

The colour of every flower Monet painted is blooming vividly in that garden. There are beds of lipstick pink tulips rising through clouds of baby blue forget-me-nots. There are many hues of pink in foxgloves and hydrangeas and banks of Busy Lizzie. There are bowers of roses over broad gravel paths and beds of blue hibiscus and flax flowers. There are purple-blue wisteria vines, in full grape-like bloom, on the humped wooden bridges. And there are waterlilies. Monet's own. Everywhere.

As a garden it was truly a work of art or, to be more exact, the work of an artist. A sight truly worthy of two eleven-hour plane trips, a day's motoring, two metro trips, a jolting hour-long train trip and fifteen minutes in a bus. It is *magnifique*.

Unfortunately, about five thousand other tourists and half a dozen school groups thought so too. I swear we have to queue to look at a flower. We are fenced out of the gravel paths. They are purely ornamental. In fact, you cannot get into the garden at all. You have to walk around the edge.

We have to queue to cross single-file under the road to visit Monet's water garden. There we follow other tourists again in single file across *la pont Japonais* and around the lake.

The sound of video cameras whirling and automatic cameras winding is deafening. But I have left my impression in France.

I reckon my bum, elbow and ears appear in, at least, fifteen thousand photographs.

We visit Monet's pink house. It has been left much as it was in Monet's time. There is a joy in the simplicity of it all. And snatched whole, as it were, from another time, you can almost hear the old man shuffling across the stone floor. But ironically the only paintings hung on the walls of Monet's own house are copies. They're prints. I smile. My spiritual journey is complete. Monet's house is just like my mother's. Full of Monet prints.

We leave the house and garden via the souvenir shop or the Monet Emporium. This is a blatant attempt by the French to Monet the world. You could buy Monet-ed anything — mugs, ties, placemats, pens. We left elated and little deluded with a Monet key ring in our pocket almost believing, 'Monet makes the world go around.'

The mother of all Eurostars

There are times when we travel as a family that the children would prefer, given the option, to jump out of a moving train into the middle of Franz Joseph Glacier, rather than suffer the excruciating embarrassment of sitting for one more minute beside their loud mother. This is one of those times.

We are travelling across France. Our first experience of the French rail system was not *fantastique*. But we learnt something of train travel, French style, second class. It is a fight to the death with American tourists for a seat.

Alas, we have another train trip planned for the following day. Eurostar, Paris to Calais, second bloody class.

'Right,' says he of the gentlemanly airs. 'I'm changing our booking. I don't care what it costs. We're going first class. We'll have reserved seats.' Of course, one can't merely upgrade. One has booked in Australia. One has to hold one's breath, whip out one's credit card and buy new tickets. And then hope that one beats the bill home. It's the only way to travel.

In preparing for this next trip I still have the storming of the Bastille in mind. We secure our luggage. We hold on tightly to our passports. I make up baguettes; nutritionally balanced baguettes. 'We'll need the sustenance to survive,' I say. 'This is a four-hour trip.'

We arrive at the Eurostar platform to be greeted by a hostess wearing a mustard suit, crisp white shirt and pert little maroon bow tie. 'May ve take your luggage?' she says.

I turn to my HRH (His Royal Happiness — he was born to travel first class). 'It sounded like English. Do you think she is talking to us?' She is. Our luggage is stowed. I immediately feel like apologising for our luggage. 'We left the Louis Vuitton at home. We are travelling light. This time we just brought the backpacks and the Billabong bum-bags.' But I don't think I'll be able to say Billabong bum-bag in French.

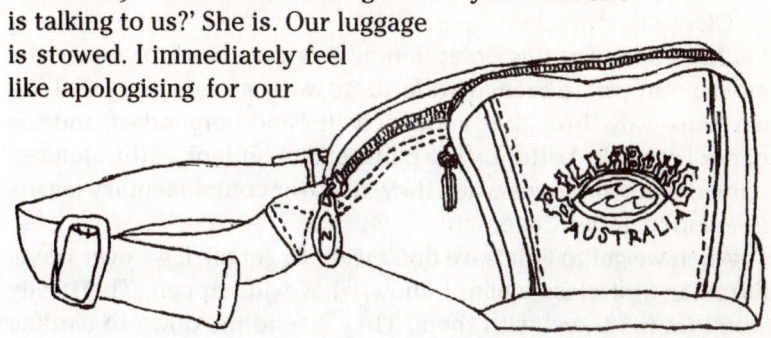

The hostess offers us our choice of newspapers and then ushers us into the quiet interior of the first-class carriage to our plush deep-purple-velvet, armchair-sized reserved seats. There is subdued lighting. There is a substantial table between the four seats. There is luxury dripping off every fitting and tap.

As the train sweeps through the French countryside, which can be viewed with pristine clarity through the vast but slightly tinted train windows, we settle down in comfort lulled by the background sound of a rhythmic railroad hum.

'Do you vish to 'ave zee meal?' asks our hostess.

'Oh. Non. Non. Merci,' I explain loudly to make up for my accent, which I'm told sounds less like French and more like a motorbike revving. 'We have baguettes — in paper bags — which we will eat,' I insist loudly, returning the razor-sharp glare of the three sets of eyes looking at me in staunch protest. And we do, as the other passengers are served three-course gourmet French meals, complete with gourmet aromas that make our saliva glands go hysterical. We eat our baguettes. They have linen. We have paper bags. They have venison. We have baguettes. The tomato is a little warm. And the lettuce a little limp. But the ham is a delight. 'It's lovely ham, isn't it?' I enthuse ignoring the venomous looks of three mumbling ingrates.

'Vould you like some vine?' asks our hostess.

'Oh. Non. Merci. We have our baguettes,' I yell.

'But zee vine is compliment-ar-y.'

'Okay.'

I have to say at this point in time it is very hard to choose the most appropriate French wine to go with a paper bag. But we work our way through several moselles and burgundies, and the paper bag looks better by the minute. The outlook of the children immediately improves when they discover complimentary means free and includes Coke.

When we get to Calais we don't want to get off. If we ever travel Eurostar first class again, I know what will happen. The family won't let me travel with them. They'll send me down to sardine second class with the baguettes.

THERE'LL ALWAYS BE AN ENGLAND and a VAT

There'll be red faces over, the White Cliffs of Dover

We leave Calais by ferry, but there is family drama afoot. The night before, Ms Stormtrooper threw up in the foyer of our hotel gasping to her obviously negligent mother between heaving breaths, 'See, I told you I was sick.'

We are booked to travel. So travel we must. But the journey between our hotel in Calais and our serviced apartment in London involves three taxi rides, two bus rides, one train trip and one long, rolling trip by ferry across the channel.

I arm myself with a stack of takeaway milkshake cartons for emergencies. I plan to deal with the situation with quiet Florence-Nightingale-type efficiency. But as we arrive at each depot, platform or taxi rank, Ms Stormtrooper, who looks and acts like a tragic waif from a Victorian stage drama, announces in a loud melodramatic voice to anyone within earshot, 'I'm sick, you know. I've thrown up five times today already.' She keeps a very accurate score. It peaks at nine. The crowds part like the Red Sea.

We are the first passengers to get on and off buses. We are whisked through customs lines like you wouldn't believe. Even the sniffer dogs were starting to dry retch.

We broke the Eurostar trip at Calais so that the children could experience the delight of seeing the white cliffs of Dover for the first time. Unfortunately, we have one sick child, one absent child (he has found the onboard video games) and it is raining. But, as we approach Dover, I track Mr Vague Teenager down. I point to the nearest rain-splattered porthole and say, 'Look at that. The white cliffs of Dover.' He puts the game on hold, looks up briefly and says those memorable words, 'Aw, yeah!' then returns to playing MarioKart. But he'll NEVER forget his mother bursting into song in public about some stupid bluebirds doing some dumb thing over those ridiculous cliffs at Dover — just you wait and see. Not that there were many people around to observe this grand lunacy. The majority of the 500-plus passengers on the Calais ferry spent the entire trip crammed together in one shopping scrum, loading up on tax-free fags and grog.

Continuing our first-class policy we book first-class seats on the train from Calais to London. We stand on the platform at Dover exuding a certain air of superior first-class smugness (between vomiting episodes). The train chugs into the station and we find we are the only passengers in the first-class carriage which is identical to the second-class carriage except for the paper sign taped on the carriage door window announcing its first-class status.

As we board the carriage, which must have reached its peak of first-class splendour in the early 1950s, we seem to have stepped into a set from 'On the Buses' with a Reg Varney lookalike and all. With blue cap, blue jacket, slightly soiled vest and fob watch, our 'Reggie' is the porter, signalman and ticket collector. Halfway through the trip, he turns into the caterer and comes whistling down the aisle with a tea trolley. We order tea with milk and Reggie manages to cheerfully shove his nicotine-stained thumbnail into every little longlife milk container he opens. 'We'll help ourselves,' we suggest. But 'No. No. No. No.' Reggie insists he will serve us. Before handing us our tea, he pulls out a rag which is so old it could have been used to flag the start of the Norman Conquests, and carefully wipes the rim of each polystyrene cup. We thank him. But we can't quite bring ourselves to drink the tea.

The little history I did at school keeps haunting me especially dramatic visions of assorted plagues like the Black Death. And, besides, when it comes to diseases, we seem to be good at self-catering.

Later that day we discover Miss Tragic Waif has tonsillitis. We pump her up with antibiotics and watch her in shifts. On the third day she starts ordering us about. Thank God. She's her old self again.

Mary, this London's a wonderful place

Finally, we arrive in the heart of London. It is like a homecoming. Everything seems so comfortably familiar. Oxford Street, Pall Mall, Bond Street, Park Lane. Of course, it is familiar, I am in a London taxi cab being driven across the Monopoly board.

I am determined to discover something of the essence of London. That's all I can hope for. You couldn't do all of London in a lifetime. There are 11 000 pubs in London alone. It would take you thirty years doing one pub a night (no Sunday's off), or only three years, if you did ten pubs a night and had a liver which deserved its own place at Madame Tussauds.

The first pub we stumble into is the quintessential London pub. The Swan has it all. A sinister history — it has been a watering hole in the 1700s for those on their way to the gallows at Marble Arch — low and menacing roof beams, polished brass beer pulls, a seriously dour publican and a typical pub menu: Sausages, Chips and Baked beans; Bacon, Chips and Baked Beans; and Fish, Chips and Baked Beans. If you want to know the true history of London, I'll tell you. Every so many years, the population of London suddenly ups and overdoses on baked beans. A typical overdose caused the Fire of London. You know, baked beans, flatulence, one spark, up she goes.

But walking the streets of London around Paddington and Mayfair has me bursting into song. With all those squares of stately terrace houses with slate roofs, and rows and rows of chimney pots, I knew where I was — in Mary Poppins territory. I could just picture Julie Andrews and Dick Van Dyck Chim-Chiminee-ing across the rooftops. Of course, these days they'd be tripping over TV aerials and satellite dishes, but the magic is still there.

I still hadn't found my idea of the essential London. I try Hyde Park. Park! It's huge. In Australia, it would be called Tasmania. Hyde Park boasts many an eccentric English tradition. First of all, there are the blue and white striped deckchairs. Ordered rows of them. But they were hire chairs: 70p for four hours, or £34 for the season. This charge amounts to an arm, a leg and a foot per season with no guarantee that the chair is pigeon pollution free.

Then there is Speaker's Corner. I could have spent hours there, listening (for a change). My favourite speaker is the Afro-Londoner — if there is such a thing — shouting, 'White men are the blight of the earth.' While the crowd, mostly white, heckle, 'If you are so smart, son, why are you wearing turquoise leather trousers?' He is. And a black Panama hat with a lime green hatband. And a long-sleeved tropical shirt.

> I try Hyde Park. Park! It's huge. In Australia, it would be called Tasmania.

I go to Westminster. I didn't expect much. I've seen those dreary Houses of Parliament images on news broadcasts from London for years. But when I step out of the underground, I stand open-mouthed, gawping in wonder. Those buildings are magnificent. The gold relief. The statuary. We never see them like that on telly. I suspect, it's the dull London light. If you picked up Big Ben and the Houses of Parliament and plonked them in, say, the Mallee on an average day, you would be blinded by their brilliance.

But I feel I still haven't discovered the essence of London. I needn't have worried. It is waiting for me in St John's Wood. That noble culture that brought us the Magna Carta has nearly eight hundred years of laws on its books. It's these laws which reflect all the history, formality and eccentricity of the culture. A very new sign at St John's Wood explains the 'By-Laws for Public Open Spaces'. I particularly like Clause 7: 'A person shall not bring into this open space any hawks, falcons or gaming birds.' Pigs, goats, cattle, sheep and beasts of burden are also banned, as are racing whippets and the sorting of rags and bones. Ditto the discharging of firearms. Naturally, they put holes in the kites.

In a square near Hyde Park children are not allowed to be unaccompanied, use the park after 6.30 p.m. or play games. What are they meant to do there? Sit and think? Another by-law states: 'It is an offence to permit a dog to foul a carriageway which is subject to a speed limit of 40 mph or less.' What does this mean? Dogs have to 'do it' on the motorway?

My favourite law dating from the 17th century allows British subjects to be buried within the bounds of their estate. And so, while we are in London, one Yorkshire chap ups and buries his dear wife in the backyard of their semi-detached. It upsets the neighbours something shocking. But it hardly causes a ripple in London. I wouldn't have been surprised if the London papers had reported the story in the gardening section under the heading 'New Ways with Compost'.

But that's London for you, in all its historical and eccentric glory.

The torture chamber (for tourists)

Of all the sights of Londontown, the Tower of London becomes for us a torturously vague recollection. We queue for three centuries in the Tower of London to check out the Crown Jewels. Finally we enter a room which doesn't contain the Crown Jewels. Just a video of the Royal Family — as if we haven't seen enough of them! — with the queue snaking backwards and forwards in corals so everyone could get a good look. At last, shuffling forward at the pace of a limping corgi, we enter another room. It doesn't contain the Crown Jewels either. Just another video. And more queuing ropes. On what feels like the Ruby Anniversary of us first entering the building, we finally hit the vault at the Tower of London to be whisked past the Crown Jewels on an escalator. But we think we saw them.

On the road again!

We are motoring out of London. Why would anyone with an intelligence level vaguely above that of a senile hedgehog want to go motoring in England? There are, after all, over twenty-two million cars in England. And, as far as Australians can work out from the world map, England would fit in the Melbourne Cricket Ground carpark.

In fact, with the English population at about fifty-eight million, Australians rather suspect they'll arrive in England to find people stacked in heaps on the pavement, while motorists take it in turns to park their cars on top of one another. But it's not like that at all. England is spacious. And it is blessed with accessible cities and endless panoramic visions of unspoilt countryside. I don't know how they do it. It may be a trick with mirrors, but England is an ideal location for a spot of serious motoring.

We head west from London along the M4. Before I can begin to describe a motoring holiday in England I must salute the English motorway system. It is an awesome feat of British engineering ingenuity. It is designed for idiots, which suits tourists. Each motorway is so clearly marked you couldn't get lost in a thick custard. Even the exits are numbered.

We roar down the M4, bore down the A303, spend what feels like the greater part of my mid-life crisis driving around in circles on the ring road near Torquay, escape and finally find ourselves chugging in a pre-war — possibly Crimean — car ferry across an estuary to Dartmouth. I have to pinch myself to make sure I haven't fallen asleep and woken up with a postcard stuck to the end of my nose. Dartmouth is a perfectly preserved Tudor village — all black wooden beams and whitewashed walls — set on a stone wharf surrounded by small boats. Yachts, these days, not fishing boats. But the effect throws you back in time.

Dartmouth is set on the river Dart with castle fortresses protecting the estuary entrance. I hadn't realised how the old sea cities were named. Exmouth is on the river — you guessed — Ex. And so on. It made me laugh. Using these principles Melbourne should really be named Yarramouth, and Perth, Swanmouth.

We are in glorious Devon. We have one week. And I want to do all the things people in Devon do. I want a Devonshire Tea. They don't have Devonshire Teas in Devonshire. I suppose they don't have manchester in Manchester either. But you can have a cream tea of cold scones, clotted Cornish cream and jam. It is delicious. But they've got it wrong, you know. They put the jam on top! Any school fete in Australia will tell you how to make a proper Devonshire Tea. Jam. Cream on top. And hot scones!

Motoring slowly through the Devon countryside is, for a middle-aged Australian, like travelling backwards through the imaginary realm of my childhood. So much of our childhood literature, from *Wind in the Willows* to *Pooh Bear*, is based on English meadows. I never really knew before what a babbling brook looked like, or a stone bridge — of the storybook kind — or buttercups or cow's parsley or bumble bees. The bumble bees amaze me. They are big, obese hairy mothers that lazily plop from one flower to the next. I could believe Devon is the place fairies hang out. It has got everything a fairy could want, bluebell hats and all.

The countryside in Devon brings tears to the amateur photographer's eyes because it's so beautiful; you can't decide which photograph to take. If you can imagine stone walls, extraordinarily steep slopes (so steep, in fact, I decided the sheep weren't chewing the grass, they were just holding on to the side of the hill with their teeth), with green pasture fitted up to the stone walls like a carpet and flowering hedgerows, then you have some idea of the beauty.

To an Australian, the hedgerows are mind-bogglingly lush. Full of hawthorn, meadow flowers, clover, ferns, ivy and anything else that can sprout a leaf. The hedgerows often start at the very edge of a single lane road and grow upwards for three metres. Driving in the back lanes of Devon was like driving through a giant maze for cars. We soon learn to wind up the windows so we don't get a swipe across the face from a straggling branch of blackberry vine or nettle. And we also learn to back up, even steep lanes. There's no choice. One of the two cars stopped bumper to bumper has to back up. It usually works fifty–fifty. But one morning we back up seven times before we stand our ground.

If touring is slow in the hedgerows, it is equally non-progressive on many of the minor A routes. It's the villages, you see. Designed for horses, they were. Not cars. Sometimes not even people. In many villages, cottage doors open directly on to the narrow, often cobbled streets. You could poke your head out your front door to see if it was safe. And lose it. I am caught in one laneway on foot with nowhere to go as a car approaches. I think I am going to end up as human jam spread across a stone wall in Stoke Fleming. But I find a nook, and the car drives past, a rear-view mirror just grazing my bustline.

Motoring through Devon is a delight, and stopping to walk some of the footpaths through the meadows was even more so. Christopher Robin (Milne, of course) actually lived much of his life near Higher Bowden in Devon. And in many woods, and many ways, he still lives there. That, you see, is the magic of Devon.

IRELAND To Be Sure, To Be Sure

On a ferry named *Felicity*

We motor through Wales to stay at Haverford West for the night before boarding the ferry for Ireland. With boarded-up shops and a hotel which reached its peak in 1625, the highlight of Haverford West is the pillar with plaque stating that William Nichol was burnt at the stake 'on this spot' in 1558. The last wild night out in Haverford West.

The next morning we leave from nearby Fishguard on a ferry named *Felicity* for a three-and-a-half-hour trip to Rosslare, Ireland. The sea is calm. The sky is blue-grey. And, with what feels like a break-through episode in the real-life family sit-com staged daily by us, we enjoy a vomit-free trip. I thank the sturdy *Felicity* from my heart as we drive our hire car out of her rear end on to the Emerald Isle.

Rosslare looks like the land that St Patrick forgot. It's blessed with a car ferry ramp and not much else. But I can tell you something about the beach at Rosslare. It has a sign. 'Bathers are advised not to walk out on or swim close to rock groynes.' Or, you might end up with a serious groyne injury, I guess! We put our toes in the water just to say we've swum in the Irish Sea, and it laps around our ankles the colour and texture of a weak iced tea.

But I am standing now on sacred ground. The home of my ancestors.

The good, the godly and the Guinness

Ireland, what is it? A tragedy set in a landscape designed for poets? Or, possibly, an island He Himself designed to fill the pages of *National Geographic* with landscapes of such breathtaking beauty they bring tears to your eyes? Or is Ireland to be found in those stretches of grey urban barrenness, so depressed, you can almost feel them sucking out your soul? Whatever it is, Ireland has it all.

I was the one who wanted to go to Ireland. The South. I didn't go specifically to trace the family roots. I wanted to go to Ireland because I grew up surrounded by Irishness. Irish nuns, holy water, guardian angels, Irish dancing, the budgie called Danny Boy, marching in St Patrick's day parades (St Patrick is revered for ridding Ireland of snakes and in my child's mind I reckoned he must have sent them to Australia), rosary beads, havin' the gift of the gab and the power of reverse logic, which is Irish to be sure, to be sure. Or unsure. Whatever.

In the land of the B&B, where every second house seems to be called The Mystical Rose, Mountain Dew or Whispering Pines, and is run by a Miss MacSweeney, I find enough Irishness to fill the heart of any young colleen. Or a middle-aged one like myself.

'What's the speed limit in Ireland?' we ask our first hostess.

'I wouldn't be knowin' that,' she replies. 'All you do is follow the car in front of you.'

'How far's the pub?' we ask.

'About tree miles. That's Irish miles mind. Just keep driving 'til you're there.'

At the pub we come across a group drowning their sorrows.

'What's up?' we ask.

'We lost the hurling,' they explain.

'Who to?'

'Oh, to ourselves,' they say and laugh.

Being interested in a bit of Guinness ourselves we think we

What St Patrick might have said

better find out the blood alcohol limit for driving in Ireland. No one knew. I ask a garda (police officer) in Limerick. He doesn't know either. The next garda replies: 'And what would you be doin' now? Askin' me an examination question?' He radios head office and, after what I suspect is some page shuffling, the answer comes back: 80 milligrams per 1000 millilitres (0.08 in our terms.) 'Now you know,' he laughs. And I suspect I am the only person in Ireland who does.

Guinness, and almost anything else that can fill a pint glass, plays a large part in Irish social life. Not sex. As Sean O'Faolin wrote: 'An Irish queer is a fellow who prefers women to drink.' Even though Guinness tastes like a thin, aerated bitumen, the Irish love it.

But they need the drink you see, to get over the food. Jesus, Mary and Holy St Joseph, Irish food must be the worst-God-given-food on this earth. And I grew up with it. I sure as hell wasn't about to travel eighteen thousand kilometres for a good feed of corned beef and cabbage. But one thing I find out in Ireland; Irish stew is not necessarily green. It was — to put it in Irish — 'Me Mam's cooking.' She killed it with frozen peas.

It is the religion that fascinates me most in Ireland. The churches and the saints. The Irish have a saint for everything. There's St Patrick, of course, patron saint of Ireland and, curiously, the patron saint of French fishermen. Perhaps it has something to do with St Patrick banning the eating of meat on Fridays for the Catholics. It must have been a boon for the French fishing industry.

Then there's St Brigid, the patron saint of dairy workers, St Gobran, patron saint of builders, and St Fiacre, patron saint of gardeners and those suffering from haemorrhoids and venereal disease! And there is also St Dymphna, patron saint of those possessed by the devil, which I suppose really means the patron saint of local government.

Yet religion has been the source of great joy and many sorrows in Ireland. Religion is not meant to interfere with the state. It does. In the Ladies room in the first pub I visit in Ireland, no condoms. They sell Mini-Mints, Smint Fresh Breath and Pretty Polly tights. I suppose tights could be a contraceptive, if tight enough. I shove HRH back into the Gents. (His Royal Hopelessness — he should have made the observation on the first visit.) Bingo! Condoms. Apparently, condoms were withdrawn in 1936 — I am trying to be delicate here — and reinstated in 1992 following an election. Next debate. Divorce. Recently passed by referendum. Just. Why? To stay in the EU (European Union) and keep those subsidies rolling in.

Oh! Ireland. What a contradiction you are! All those centuries of fighting the English — and each other — for independence. You get it in 1938. And in the 1990s you are ruled by Brussels! The bogs must sigh at night and the stones weep.

If you ever go across the sea to Youghal

Motoring through County Cork on the southern shores of Ireland, we stop at the small seaside village of Youghal. We find Youghal is a very historical town.

Sir Walter Raleigh's 16th-century house is there. It's said he planted the very first potatoes in Ireland in that very garden. Cromwell's Arch is said to be where the conqueror exited the city walls and sailed from Ireland in 1656.

There's a historical plaque recording the names of the great men who have passed through the city gates including Sir Walter Raleigh, Cromwell and Gregory Peck. Gregory Peck? The film *Moby Dick* was shot at Youghal in 1954. And I'm sure even Gregory Peck would have been surprised to find himself written into the history books of Ireland. Let's face it, he was no great conqueror. He didn't even beat the whale.

And how much might Jesus be costing, now?

The trip through the south of Ireland with the family becomes for me a journey through the shadowlands of my own heart.

I was brought up a Catholic in Australia, and I inherited bog Irish Catholicism where souls floated footless and bewildered in purgatory until a seven-year-old said a decade of the rosary on All Saints Day to save those souls from eternal confusion, and where guardian angels hovered over your shoulder to protect you except when you fell off your bike.

The most tangible symbol of this Catholicism in my childhood family was a statue of Jesus. The plaster statue of a curly-locked boy Jesus with the gold-trimmed blue robes and the exposed sacred heart stood, frozen in blessing, on a four-legged mahogany pedestal in Nanna and Papa O'Donnell's bedroom for all of my early life.

I'd tippy toe into the bedroom to look reverently at Jesus. He was as sacred in my childhood as he had been in my mother's.

And there Jesus remained for over two decades of my life. In his sacred place, secure and respected, until my grandparents died and we had to clear out the house.

My grandparents' room remained as it had always been in my childhood. Unchanged. But I had changed and so had the rest of my family. Catholicism had taken a battering in twenty-odd years. We'd bolted from our guardian angels and they never caught up with us again!

But there stood Jesus still surveying his shadowy domain. My mother bustled in behind me and gasped, 'OH, my God. What are we going to do with Jesus?' Something had to be done.

My mother, Kathleen, despite her recent investigation of Eastern religions couldn't bring herself to dethrone Jesus. I did. I took him off his pedestal and set him on the carpet.

My mother and I, as if we'd done enough heretic business for one day, then busied ourselves with cleaning and sorting the rest of the house. We giggled with the idiocy (my grandparents had thrown out the best mahogany furniture, but saved all their false teeth) and wiped the occasional tear from our eyes as we attempted to clean two lifetimes out of the house. Meanwhile, my younger sister Joanne, an explosion of seven-year-old toothless energy in jeans and Strawberry Shortcake T-shirt zipped around the house. My mother had stopped yelling 'Don't!' and let my sister play havoc as was the tone of the day.

We, the senior women, were working our way under the kitchen sink when my sister hop-glided into the kitchen on one roller-skate carrying Jesus.

'Mum,' she enthused. 'Can I take this out the back and knock its block off?' Jesus, the all holy, had become a mere object to the youngest member of the third generation. An innocuous 'it'.

'No,' snapped mother, adding, 'Be careful. Don't drop ...' Too late. Jesus hit the green-flecked linoleum with a thud and broke his arm. Our mother picked up the bits of Jesus and fixed his arm with a bandaid as my sister zipped off on one roller-skate looking for alternative amusement.

'Mum,' I snorted, 'That looks ridiculous. We are talking the Son of God here. In bandaids. Throw him out.'

She couldn't. She wrapped Jesus in an old eiderdown and took him home to Kyneton, a small town one hundred kilometres from Melbourne. Jesus lived in her cupboard for five years and ended his life, following one cleaning frenzy, on the Kyneton tip.

Memories of Catholicism and rebellion and Jesus had settled as sludge at the bottom of my memory banks under the general category of 'To be sorted later'. And there the memories sat slowly petrifying for two decades until I walked in a shop in Youghal. It was a shop that sold rosary beads, plastic crucifixes, bibles and first holy communion cards. And it looked like a bigger version of the stall run by the good ladies of St Kevin's Parish Church after 10.30 a.m. mass on the Sundays of my childhood.

But what had drawn me into the shop was the statue of Jesus in the window. The same Jesus. The same curly locks and exposed sacred heart. The same mould. The same paint.

And I had to ask, 'How much is Jesus?'

'Aw,' scoffed the matronly shop assistant with such a massive bust she had to almost lift it by hand so she could take each breath, 'he wouldn't be for sale now, would he? Not Jesus. He'd be priceless.'

And I couldn't help but reflect on the fate of Jesus, so different in two different lands. In one country he's priceless. And in another place across the sea he ended his days twenty years ago on the local tip.

It seemed to me that all the religious fervour that came out to Australia with the Irish, especially the nuns and priests, had somehow slipped into the cracks of a dry land and dissipated. For we are not a religious country, Australia. Few of us, statistics say, ever go to church.

This thought slithered quickly through my brain like a snake on a walking track, for the matronly one soon brought me back to consciousness with the further comment: 'But Mary here is for sale. She's lovely, only £39.'

And she was lovely. To be sure. I explained that I was travelling and couldn't fit the one-metre Mary into my hand luggage. There was another statue, too; over one metre long and fully 3-D. The Last Supper. It was hand-painted, with the eyes ever so slightly out of whack suggesting a serious chromosomal deficiency had beset all the apostles. I tell you, I was tempted. But I left the shop empty-handed and a little hollow at heart.

We pressed on to Limerick, where there was one last religious evocation awaiting me. Having my religious curiosity aroused in Youghal, I thought I should see what a Catholic church looked like in Ireland. Not a cathedral. Just an ordinary local church. I saw one in Limerick and called to the family as I crossed the road, 'I'm just going to have a quick look inside the church.'

As I clutched the brass handle and, with effort, pulled open the carved wooden doors, I stepped back in time into my childhood, into the churches of my childhood.

> With the eyes slightly out of whack – it suggested a serious chromosomal deficiency had beset all the apostles.

It was all there: the solid oak pews; the hard wooden kneelers; the confessionals; the stained glass windows; the stations of the cross; the marble altar with the plaster figure nailed to a wooden cross above; the communion banister; and the grottos. The grotto on the left held the statue of the Sacred Heart of Christ, the adult Christ in red robes with the candle flickering under the red cut-glass lid. To the right, Mary the Immaculate in blue robes with the candle flickering under the blue cut-glass lid. Fresh flowers were arranged in vases. The smell of incense lingered. It was my childhood. I was a little girl again in the black patent-leather shoes, short sox, and the lemon dress with the sash and the sailor's hat. And this little person wanted to genuflect and put her hand, her much smaller hand, into the holy water and bless herself and kneel to tell Jesus that he hasn't sorted out the world yet. She wanted him to because everyone told her to believe in him. And she did then.

But a wave of fear took hold of me. There was something lurking in the shadows of the church. Guilt. I remembered the guilt. The guilt about everything. The sins. The big sins were mortal sins. The little ones, venal sins. In my Catholic childhood almost anything you did had a sin attached.

I ran out of the church and down the hill to my family. It was a knee-jerk reaction. I didn't stop to think about the moral code Catholicism had given me on which, if nothing else, I could base a debate. Or the changes that had taken place in the Catholic church in more recent times. I just ran as fast as I could to get away from the guilt before it grabbed me and held me captive again.

The experience showed me that I had found some sense of freedom in my own mind and I wasn't going back. Saints be praised!

Blessed saints and sinners

We leave Limerick and follow the wide and graceful Shannon River as far as we can until we take the turn-off towards Dublin. But before we reach Dublin we take a leisurely motoring tour of the Wicklow Mountains. There we make four intriguing discoveries.

Firstly we find the bogs. Real bogs. Black, spongy, cracked and crumbling peatlands. We all clamber out of the car and half spring and half walk about the bogs among the short spindly bushes. And we fall down the cracks because some of the cracks are as wide as a gaping grave, and almost as deep. There is a wild and eerie feel to the bogs. The shrill wind cries, and the earth hisses, for there are ghosts trapped here in every layer of peat.

Further down the road we see the bogs being harvested for peat. Stripped almost bare. Some say one day the bogs will be gone; all burnt as fuel. And I felt like standing in the middle of the magical bogs and yelling, 'This is dead gorgeous. You wouldn't want to be wrecking it now.'

Next we discover that not all saints are fascinating people. Some are quite dull. St Kevin, for instance, would make it on to the 100-Most-Boring-People-in-World list. He was a hermit. This did not deter me, however. 'Visit the hermit saint's beehive stone cell at Glendalough,' it said in the brochure. A must-see for the tourist. I thought I would but it nearly killed me.

I leave the family complaining in the car, run up the mountain, past a picnic area, past church ruins and past three mountain sheep, stub my toe twice, catch my hair on a low lying tree branch and find it. About three stones remain. St Kevin — I know who he is now: the patron saint of gullible tourists.

After all this excitement and expenditure of effort I have to find a toilet. I do. But if you make it to Glendalough, I have a tip for you. Don't get caught behind the Kilmanargh Twirling Troop in the women's toilets. They are wearing so many white petticoats and green and orange overskirts and green hair ribbons and white hair ribbons with hair nets and hair buns, there is no way of actually penetrating through the group to get to a toilet cubicle. I am stuck two metres from the toilet cubicle not knowing who to pray to — who the patron saint of bladder control is! Only minutes from dying of a ruptured bladder, I finally find relief in Glendalough and plod exhausted back to my waiting family who are obviously thinking anything but saintly thoughts as they sit nearly dislocating their respective jaws practising sour looks.

The final discovery we make in the Wicklow Mountains is that a healthy whiff of good old country air is not always all that it's cracked up to be. We are in a farming area where one whiff is enough and two whiffs could be fatal.

It is slurry season. Farm animals are barned in the winter months in Europe. The manure is collected, then, I suspect, fermented and finally sprayed on the fields in spring. I am all for sucking in that country air but this smell was unbelievable. I feel as though we'd gone to bed one night and woken the next day to discover the whole of Ireland had turned into a high-strength cowpat.

It is so strong in this area each breath makes you feel as if you are fertilising your nostrils and plants will sprout at any minute out of your ears.

'God! God! I can taste it in the air,' shouts Miss Blunt-And-To-The-Point as she sprints yet again from the car to the safety of indoors holding her hand over her mouth in case she vomits. 'Crap,' replies the teenage Master of Grunge. 'Yes,' retorts his sister. Leaving the argument much in confusion.

I tell you, after the slurry, there was nothing like taking a good deep gulp of city pollution in Dublin to make us all feel better. But we are not staying in Dublin long. There is just enough time to salute the statue of Michael Collins — the architect of Irish Independence — then catch the next ferry for Wales.

THIS IS WALES, BOY-O!

Wales arrives with a jumble of confusion on the road signs and a steady climb into the craggy mountains, once home to the fierce Celts, who, so we are told, fought various invaders — Normans and Saxons — naked!

It is the road signs which cause the greatest angst to the novice tourer. Welsh is a language in which every word constitutes a small opera sung by people overwhelmed with a need to clear their throats every second syllable.

To give you an idea, the first road sign in Wales we stumble on is for 'Services' on the motorway, which in Welsh is *Gwasanaethau*. This would not be so bad, except for the fact that the Welsh are fiercely patriotic. Road signs are in Welsh. TV programmes are run in Welsh. In fact, during our stay a girl is sacked from the BBC for saying on a kindergarten programme in Welsh, 'Do not stand on the balloons or Big Ted will be pissed off,' the last two words in English. And I'm not sure if she is sacked for using swear words, or English.

As a consequence of this patriotism, Welsh appears above the English on road signs in equal-sized type. Thus as you approach a sign, which says, somewhere, in English 'Road narrows to single lane on bridge,' you find yourself still plodding through the Welsh when you are already on the bridge hurtling towards an unsympathetic lorry.

> The locals are sunbaking on a pebble beach. I'm talking about pebbles the size of a decent potato.

Welsh-bred HRH (His Royal Happiness) is relishing being back on his home turf pointing out the highlights like his old house, his other old house, and his old school, as the children fall asleep in the back seat, and I utter 'Yes, darling' every so often while reading a book. At one stage though, HRH, who has so far shown no inclination to fight naked though I am prepared to wait, and myself, are at each other's throat over the road signs. He feels yet again I am not paying due attention, while I feel hurtling past them at 100 mph on the M4 between two lorries gives me little chance. I am trying to find the town called 'ethy ydv' on the map. He accuses me of losing us again. But three signs later I find out it isn't my Welsh that is the problem. We are on the road to Methyr Tydvil, it is only a few letters had fallen off the road sign.

Wales seems to me to be the undiscovered gem of the United Kingdom. It's not that other parts of Britain are not beautiful but they've been discovered. If you're not knee-deep in Australian tourists, you are being run down by a determined group of touring Swedish youth. But Wales was just there getting on with business.

In the south, there are towns and cities, gripped by the sprawling monotony of urban depression. The wail of the coal mine siren in the 1940s has been replaced in the '90s with the creaking sound of rusted cranes on the waterfront, for the docks are abandoned and still. There's no place for coal now.

Barry, the birth-town of my boy-o, is a case in point. It is in some ways a sad homecoming. Shops are closed in the high street. Houses unchanged from the '40s — not even for a coat of new paint. But, you know, they survive.

It is in Barry that I see some of the whitest people I've seen on this earth. One shouldn't stare, but they looked badly in need of a pint of blood. Even so, the locals are determined, mind, to get some sun. Sunbaking, they are, on a pebble beach. I'm talking about pebbles the size of a decent potato. You put your towel down, and then you lie on it. I don't know how you get comfortable, but these are the sacrifices made by determined Celtic stock each summer to become a darker shade of pale.

Nearby Barry Island is still the resort town for those who like the annual trip to Butlins for a break. Butlins has gone. It's the Barry Island Resort now. Real posh. But you can still get your pony-ride on the beach for 50p and play bingo. The bingo is electronic now. Put in 10p and the numbers light up. And they call a game every five minutes. You pull these sliding covers across the numbers and bingo if you're lucky.

It is north Wales though that wins our hearts. Snowdonia, with its harsh and stony foothills leading up to shale-covered mountains and knife-edge peaks, seems so frozen in time you can almost hear the bloodthirsty cries of the fighting Welsh princes echoing in the valleys. We just have to stop and stare in wonder at the stone fences which seem to run straight up an almost vertical cliff face and disappear. We stand and wonder why anyone would bother. A sheep couldn't climb up there armed with pitons, and, besides, it would be grazing in shale.

Then you descend into a valley with a lake cut from glass and a village straight out of a storybook with babbling brook, stone bridge and a post office. And all of this surrounded by hillsides cushioned with pillows of wild rhododendrons. It is so beautiful your thumb is worn weary taking the photographs.

And always Wales turns on the unexpected. Safeway Petrol: we thought they'd be filling the car up with yoghurt. Sheep roaming around the hillsides and parking themselves in the carpark. And wind farms — you would turn a corner to come across these surreal white monsters in banks of twenty or more turning rhythmically on the barren hilltops.

But the fierce Celt spirit lives on. The Welsh need it to survive the food. The bara frwyth (fruit bread) and cage bach (Welsh cakes) are a delight. But Laver bread is the go in Wales says, my boy-o. You could kill yourself with English breakfasts touring England and Wales. You know, an overdose of cholesterol. But do breakfast right in Wales and you'll be having fried eggs, fried black pudding, fried sausages and fried Laver Bread. It is made of seaweed and oatmeal and it tastes like gourmet slime. By God, those Celts are tough.

SCOTLAND: Land of Lochs and Rocks
Four! (And that's just a golfer's IQ)

We fly into Scotland on a Midlands service. I stand at Bag Collection Bay No. 2 in Edinburgh Airport fascinated by the emerging luggage. I've never seen so much hope and frustration collected in one location. I'm looking at a revolving bevy of golf clubs. Bag after bag of hope. Golfers, having their major handicap located between the ears, arrive in buoyant groups to play golf in Scotland all the time hoping it won't rain. This, in the country that invented rain! I also see bag after bag of frustration. Golf is, as far as I can work out, an unnatural act invented by sadists, to keep masochists happy.

There's nothing quite so heady as the smell of Burger King in the morning

It is Sunday morning in Edinburgh and we need to buy something desperately: an umbrella. We are, of course, as idiotically optimistic as every other holiday-goer. We travel to Scotland without umbrellas. Even the telltale signs at the airport didn't dampen our optimism. There are umbrella stands at every doorway and a covered walkway to the hire car!

We walk around Edinburgh and the rain pours down around us in a mixture of horizontal and vertical sheets. There are three shops open — Burger King, Pizza Hut, and the Disney Shop. There is a moral to this story. As Robbie Burns said, or would have said given the chance, 'If at first you don't succeed, franchise.'

Scotland is a land of great contrasts, especially for the tourist. We visit Edinburgh Castle. It stands a hauntingly beautiful monument to fortitude and royal blood lines. However, 500 000 tourists visit Edinburgh (Pop. 422 000) each year, and between me and Edinburgh Castle stand the entire 500 000, give or take a few. And it is raining cats and dogs, or spats and sporrans; this is Scotland.

We wander around the back of Edinburgh Castle. In the cemetery we find a little brass plaque dedicated to the mathematician John Napier, 1550–1617. In a previous life, in my twenties, I was a mathematics teacher. John Napier invented logarithms. He is the one of the founding father's of modern mathematics. And he gets a little brass plaque. Grey Friars Bobby gets an entire statue in Edinburgh. But the inventor of logarithms gets a plaque. There is a moral to this story, boys and girls. You will get more recognition in this world by being cute and friendly, than by becoming a mathematician.

Next we head to the nearby souvenir shops though we are soon McTartaned out. No wonder. They sell tartan everything — playing cards, bagpipe back-scratchers, clan tea towels, hedgehogs in kilts, rabbits in tartan pants, and whisky-flavoured McCondoms (see Duncan for a demo). But, at least, now I know what a Scotsman wears under his kilt.

We drive out of Edinburgh to Scone, which is pronounced to rhyme with 'phone'. It makes sense. We have bone, stone, alone, zone. Why not Scone? But we also have done and none. So why not 'Scun'? It's a ridiculous language, English. No wonder they can hardly speak it in Scotland!

There in Scone, resting in the full glory of an aristocratic estate, is Scone Palace. It has it all. The porcelain, the ivories, the 18th-century clocks, the tea rooms, the souvenir shop (they do a lovely line in Scone jams), the vast grounds, and freedom to roam. The appeal of Scone is, however, that the Earl still lives there. The family snaps are on display. Grandma. Grandpa. Mum. Dad. Wedding photos. Baby snaps. The kids in the bath. It is like watching 'Neighbours' set in a palace.

> The first mug was released in 1838. That's who started merchandising: the Royal Family.

From Scone we motor north heading for Queen Victoria's little summer holiday retreat, Balmoral Castle. It is an elegant house festooned with a bloom of stag horns; not ferns, real ones. They are everywhere. Hanging in the Great Hall and filling every space under the stable eaves. I was beginning to suspect that the local deer must be born with a mounting board behind their neck.

More surprisingly, housed inside the stables is the full collection of commemorative china. The first mug was released in 1838 to commemorate Queen Victoria's coronation. That's who started merchandising: the Royal Family. They did it first.

Since then almost the entire history of the Royal Family is recorded in mugs and plates. All the weddings. Charles and Diana's wedding — four mugs and a plate. Sarah and Andrew's marriage — three mugs and one plate. Anne's marriage to Mark Phillips — one mug. Her second marriage — not even a teaspoon.

Standing gazing at the china, I couldn't help but ponder the opportunities missed. This is a family acquainted with ritual. For the wedding — a commemorative plate. For the divorce — why not a ritual smashing of the plate? I must write a letter to the Queen.

Meanwhile, it is at Balmoral that I run into my first fully blown hallucination. Or is it?

How to distinguish a hallucination from a photo opportunity

I must digress for a moment and ponder on the mind-distorting nature of the photo opportunity. If you find yourself standing agog anywhere in the world unable to believe your own eyes, there are three simple steps you need to follow to determine whether you are looking at a hallucination or, indeed, a photo opportunity.

Step 1
Ask yourself, 'Is this hallucination being affected by the weather?' In a hallucination, the naked nymph, say, dancing through Hyde Park with the psychedelic butterflies will rarely be seen carrying an umbrella or, for that matter, putting on sunglasses and sun hat. Thus a show of sun hats or umbrellas means reality prevails and you can take home a snap of yourself dancing with the psychedelic butterflies. If still in doubt continue to Step 2.

Step 2
Turn to the person beside you and ask them if they would kindly do the honours and photograph you dancing with the psychedelic butterflies. If they say 'yes', you are dealing with an A-grade photo opportunity.

If that person looks at you as if your head has just exploded, you are in trouble (especially if the person beside you turns out to be a lamp-post.) Proceed to Step 3.

Step 3
What the hell, go and dance with the psychedelic butterflies anyway. If you are arrested, and put into a jacket with very long sleeves then you have your answer. It is a hallucination!

Such is the nature of travel, so bizarre, so out-of-context, so unbelievable are certain visions in unexpected places, you stand there, flabbergasted, wondering if you have serious jet lag psychosis or have just overdosed on the refresher towels. In such cases despite the persistence of reality, it still makes more sense to question your own mental stability than accept the truth.

I am crunching down the gravel pathway out of Balmoral Castle revelling in the glory of a Scottish summer day. The river Dee babbles. The grand old oaks scatter motley shade across the path, and the lawn beside the castle stretches out like a fifty-hectare green carpet to the edge of the shaded woods.

I am overcome with an urge to go don a deerstalker hat and plus-fours and go out and shoot something myself. It must have been something in the air, or the sight of all those fabulous antlers hanging around the stables speaking of the days when men hunted and women knew what to do with a good set of antlers.

However, the thought of joining a royal hunt party vanishes in one step. I stand in front of a memorial to the war dead of Balmoral and gawp. It is covered in swastikas. Swastikas!

My mind is filled with wild imaginings along the lines of, 'My God! Queen Victoria must have been Hitler's mother?' I am almost convinced there is a likeness especially about the hair until I read a notice beside the memorial. The swastika has been used for centuries in many cultures to symbolise life and abundance. In Sanskrit, the swastika symbolises peace. It also appears on the spine of Rudyard Kipling's first editions.

The memorial in question was erected after the First World War when the swastika was, in fact, still a symbol of hope. Later it was hijacked by the Nazis and forever branded evil.

It's a great tribute to historical accuracy that the memorial remains. But for those Balmoral locals whose sons and daughters died fighting the Nazis it must have been hard to stomach.

If you drink enough whisky, the haggis tastes good!

I always wanted to go to Scotland because I had such an eccentric vision of the place. In my mind, Scotland was a rugged land populated by a Celtic cross between Billy Connolly and Mel Gibson's Braveheart. Surely the moment I set foot in Scotland some wild-eyed, kilt wearing warrior would come charging toward me and tell me a joke. Amazingly enough, this eccentric vision is 'nae sae far from the trewth'. Scotland proves to be a land of extraordinary contrasts.

The humour is there. 'Och aye! We all need a wee laugh, noo and agin!' which may explain the Loch Ness monster discovered, sort of, in 1933. It has had the Scots laughing and raking in the tourist pounds ever since. They have a museum and all.

There is humour in the local tales. Did you hear about the dignitary who opened a speech in Glasgow with the words, 'I was born an Englishman. And I will die an Englishman,' to be upstaged by a Glaswegian yelling, 'Have you no ambition, mon?'

The savagery is there too. All over Scotland, history is written in clan blood. After Balmoral we drive to Inverness and on to the battlefields of Culloden.

And there is no more harrowing an experience than to stand on the moor at Culloden where in 1746 Bonnie Prince Charlie's supporters were slaughtered by the English and others, clan against clan. To stand on that moor on a day of sleeting rain, much as it was in 1746, was to hear the battlefield echo with the death cries of the clans. And of Scotland too, for independence was lost on that day. Ah, yes! There is a Scottish Government now, but it's ruled from 10 Downing Street. That's nae the same as independence. Ask the Irish!

Yet there is black humour to be found in this macabre story. Scots have always been great sports fans. Many locals turned up on that day to watch the battle. You can just imagine the local gossip. 'Aye. O'er the moor. A warld match. Scotland versus England. We'll kill twa at a blow.' But they were slaughtered. Spectators too!

There are many more contrasts to be found in Scotland. I thought the landscape would be all great drama and poetry. And it is, in places. Other areas boast gentle picture-book meadows and cottage farmhouses. I could see why golf began in Scotland. The grass in some meadows is so smooth, so green, the farms look like golf courses. All a farmer had to do was walk back from the field with a stick, and hit a rock! Bingo! Golf was invented. And some of us have never improved the standard since that day.

Then there is Scotch whisky. By serious sampling of the local product, I find whisky comes in startlingly different varieties. I also learn how to describe a whisky. For instance, 'a sweet, light, nutty single highland malt' tastes like two-stroke motor fuel rinsed through the bits the haggis rejects, while 'a smoky, grassy, fruity single malt' means it tastes like burnt socks aged in aeronautical fuel mix. And, by God, the taste grows on you. The burning of the tonsils may explain that accent.

From Inverness we drive to the Isle of Skye. I recall the song 'Speed Bonnie Boat like a Bird on the Wind' because Skye is a miracle of permanence; it's a wonder it hasn't been totally eroded by wind centuries ago. It's springtime and standing on the shores of Skye I think my nose could be blown off my face. But there is a wild barreness about the island that appeals to my Celtic heart.

From Skye we drive back to London. And it rains the whole way. I begin to believe they have installed a faulty sprinkler system in the sky. But this is Scotland.

Glorious Scotland. And long may she rain.

ITALY or How Hard Can Life Be in a Villa in Tuscany?

Friends, Romans and countrymen, we're on our way!

Italy is an aberration in our itinerary, an opportunity. Friends say 'Go! Go to Italy. We'll look after the kids.' Almost before they have finished this last sentence and definitely before they are declared legally insane by the local health authority, HRH and I grab our bags and go.

In the magic realm

We fly into Rome, eat a pizza at 8 a.m. because I can't wait to try an Italian pizza, and the verdict: my taste buds don't wake up until 10 a.m. so I'm none the wiser. We catch a train to Pisa where we have arranged to meet friends from Australia. So well-synchronised are mobile phone links and satellites that we talk to them via Australia from our Italian train as they drive over the Swiss Alps. When our train pulls into the station at Pisa they are standing outside our carriage still talking to us on the mobile phone. I don't know why we didn't stay home and talk to each other over the phone for twenty cents.

We drive to our villa, and I find myself in Tuscany looking down through a summer haze to the Garfagnane Valley below where the small village of Castelnuovo is trapped in permanent tranquillity between the high drama of the Apuane Alps on the one side and the Apennines on the other. And I am drunk on the magnificence of the Tuscan landscape.

Of course, the several bottles of chianti I seem to have spontaneously consumed on my arrival at the villa have helped the intoxication of my senses. But Tuscany, oh Tuscany, I can understand now why you have seduced generations of poets and writers, painters and scientists. With your terraced olive groves and terracotta roofs, with your walled cities and white marble cathedrals, with your stone bridges and pink villas with green window shutters and red geraniums overflowing window boxes, you, Tuscany, are a magic realm.

Like writers who have come to Tuscany before me, Alan Moorehead, Virginia Woolf, Dylan Thomas, Dostoevsky and Aldous Huxley, I have come to stand where the great masters stood — Giotto, Michelangelo, Leonardo Da Vinci, Botticelli, to name a few — and breathe in deep draughts of inspiration through the mystical air. And so, it's to Florence we must go.

We rise early, and kitted out in suntan lotion, sunglasses and sandals, we leave for Florence in a bevy of excitement. Five minutes into our two-and-a-half-hour journey to Florence, my romantic vision was bulldozed flat by a near-death experience with a Lamborghini bus. Or, at least, it was a bus that thought it was a Lamborghini. The four of us in the car all held our breath to give the bus just that little bit more room to squeeze past us at great speed in a narrow street. I tell you, driving around the back roads of Italy is like driving through Dante's *Inferno* in a hire car. Rumour has it that Italians drive on the right-hand side of the road. This is not true. From our experience, the Italians have not yet decided which side of the road they drive on. They like them both.

Assumed translation of road sign

KEEP RIGHT
KEEP LEFT
WHATEVER

And to read a map of Italy you actually need occult skills. Advising the driver to turn left, was, at times, like saying, 'Ah, yes. You've just turned up the death card in Tarot. It's a one-way street, the other way.'

But despite the roads, despite the maps and despite the packs of Vespa drivers that seemed to buzz around us at times like swarms of killer bees, we make it to Florence. We park the car outside the old city and prepare to walk into the centre of Florence to be seduced by the grand artistry of the Renaissance architecture.

But first we need a toilet. We find one. It is a toolshed. We ask for help. A girl on a Vespa points to a toilet. It is locked. We bolt along the Arno River walkway suddenly very interested in Toilet Architecture. We find a Porta-loo. Yellow. Vaulted plastic roof. Moulded door. Contemporary handle. It is the most magnificent building I have seen in Florence. But it is locked too.

I am prepared to sprint into the heart of Florence and incorporate myself in Neptune's Fountain for relief. Fortunately, and just in time, we find the toilet block in some public baths. I can only say, when in Rome do as the Romans do, but when in Florence do it when you can, you may not get a second chance.

Finally, we are there. I stand outside the Santa Maria Del Fiore duomo (cathedral) breathless. Its white marble gives it a hauntingly ghost-like appearance as if it were on loan from some celestial civic group. The experience inside the cathedral is so spiritually intense I am a little worried I will see visions, although, I suspect, I'd blow any grab at sainthood by asking for the lotto numbers!

Now to the great works of art. First Michelangelo's David. We trot off to the Uffizi. It is shut. We look up the other museums. They are shut too, the whole twenty-four of them, because it is a Monday. We have travelled fifteen thousand kilometres to turn up on the day Florence was shut. 'But I need inspiration,' I gasp.

All is not lost. I do see some great works of art in street stalls. Raphael's cupids on a jewel box lid. Botticelli's *Birth of Venus* on a genuine T-shirt. And Michelangelo's David on a barbecue apron. Now, that is inspiring. David's a man of the modern era. He slays giants then dons the apron and chucks a few scaloppine on the barbie. Ciao!

Closed for repair

The next day, market day in Castelnuovo, our efforts to speak Italian prove to be of great entertainment value for the locals. In one cafe, three of us order cappuccino and one of us a *latte*. She gets it too. A glass of milk. I can't laugh, I think *latte* is coffee too.

When I order some prosciutto ham at a deli the shop assistant looks at me as if I'd been voted district *idiota* of the month, with good reason. Prosciutto means ham in Italian. I've been ordering 'ham' ham in Australia for years. But my best effort is calling the *carabinieri* the 'carbonara'. If I was mugged, I wouldn't be yelling for the police. I would be screaming to be saved by a cream sauce!

Italians are passionate about food. Cardinal Tonini of Ravenna recently complained that Italians no longer consider sins of the flesh to be sins, but rather 'errors'. But it would be a sin in Italy to use canned muck in your cooking. Tomatoes aren't grown in Italy. They are lovingly reared like members of the family.

The food in Italy is fresh, fragrant and seductive. The pastas and the pizzas are *magnifico*. Some fool in Australia told me Italian pizzas were ordinary. I should track them down and beat them to death with an anchovy for being so stupid. I had pizzas in Italy which made some of the Aussie efforts I have tried taste like Bathmat Margherita.

And the gelati. Oh! The gelati! Chocolato. Tira-misu. Bacci. I'll have to join GA soon. Gelati Anonymous. Just so that I don't explode.

But the grand passion for Italians, possibly the grandest, involves *vino*. And you can see this passion carved into the hillsides of the Cinque Terre. This is our first grand adventure since the Florence fiasco. We check guidebooks, wind speeds and astrology charts. We should have no trouble.

We drive out of the coastal village of Portovenere up and up and up. The road twists, turns, narrows. I'm talking serious lack of road shoulder. A ribbon of bitumen. Hundreds of metres of sheer drop to the sea and I'm suffering from terminal vertigo. The view is spectacular. I could have vomited into the Mediterranean from 330 metres. Or more. At one stage we face a road sign with '15' on it. 'My God,' moans one of our party. 'The road is narrowing to fifteen centimetres.' It doesn't. It is merely a 15 kph bend. That's beyond hairpin. It's a kidney twister!

Yet along these precipitous valleys and vast cliff faces plunging to the sea, there are grapevines planted. So steep are these vineyards, you cannot see the vines from the road. How they harvest these grapes, I don't know. They must absail or wear parachutes to pick grapes in the Cinque Terre. I swear, if the Italians owned the Grand Canyon it would be planted with vines. That's some passion for the grape. So I drink to the Italians. But only on flat earth.

Poetry in (body language) motion

We drive over the last thin band of road clinging to the great precipices of the Riviera di Levante cliffs down into the seaside town of Levanto, and catch a train to the fishing village of Manarola. There we enter a world of total enchantment. Manarola is a fishing village where three- and four-storey pink and lemon villas are built on the rocks and cliff faces of the *Golfo dei Poeti* (Gulf of the Poets). The Mediterranean dances below us, an ocean of sparkling blue liqueur, while children perch on rocks and jump squealing directly into the rippling sea.

The most stunning aspect of Manarola is that, in the land of the Lamborghini, the streets here are too steep and narrow for cars. It is a pedestrian's paradise. We stroll through the village and along the beach pathway drunk on the heady romance of the setting. And more than a little heady from a couple of bottles of Sciacchetra, the local white wine. We feel we are so familiar with local grape-growing techniques, that we should sample some of the product of the vine.

It is while strolling along the beach pathway linking the villages of the Cinque Terre that I learn more of the Italian method communication. The full body technique.

One of the great spectacles of Italy involves watching Italians being themselves. Wherever two or more Italians are gathered passion flows. And overflows. At one stage, one of our party of four is pinched on the bum: HRH (His Royal Heterosexualness) And he's been very smug since!

But Italian is a language of passion. It can take many words, hand gestures, sighs, grunts and operatic facial expressions to say 'maybe'. It takes a three-act play and two intervals to order a bottle of wine. Gossiping requires, in the telling and retelling, every inch of the body and extra effort from the eyebrows.

Somehow in moving from a beach path to a clifftop walkway

and back again we become lost. An enthusiastic local gives us directions, which we don't understand. But from his hand gestures I gather that we are to go over several mountains, under a bridge, turn left, make love, have a good stretch, tell a few jokes, turn left at the winery and we'll be there.

Cheerfully following his directions we soon find ourselves walking into the echoing, slimy-walled gloom of a one kilometre-long railway tunnel. Mid-tunnel I think I will get my throat slit for the contents of my backpack, which consists of one pair of wet bathers and a Visa card two hundred dollars short of total meltdown. At the end of the tunnel we finally find out what the obliging Italian has been trying to tell us, namely: 'You go through this bloody awful tunnel, to the hippy commune where they smoke dope and bath naked under an irrigation pipe, then turn right, climb the narrow donkey track until one of your party has a heart attack, is buried on the hill and then you're almost there.' Needless to say, we walk the one kilometre back through the tunnel of death, and arrive back where we started, much to our relief.

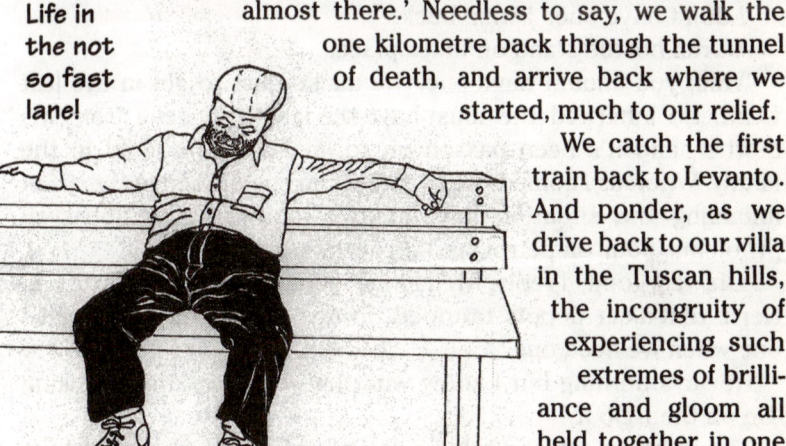

Life in the not so fast lane!

We catch the first train back to Levanto. And ponder, as we drive back to our villa in the Tuscan hills, the incongruity of experiencing such extremes of brilliance and gloom all held together in one magic day — our last day in Italy.

WE GOIN' HOME!

Back in London, we're preparing for that muscle-numbing marathon of zombied out discomfort: twenty-four hours of airflight. We are going home to Australia.

I find packing for home after a long trip is easy. I instruct children to take out the least dirty socks they own and put them on. Ditto least dirty top, jeans and jumper. We look like refugees from a bargain basement war. HRH looks impeccable. He pays so much to have his smalls laundered by an express overnight service, his underpants have now earned enough frequent flier points to take a holiday in the Bahamas on their own.

We scoop up all the souvenirs, knick-knacks, extra clothes, used film cartridges, gifts, additional maps, travel guides and duty-free bargains and ruthlessly squash them into twice the number of bags we arrived with, while shoving leftover bits into bulging plastic carrybags. We take a last, an extra last, and one more last look around our rooms to make sure we have packed everything and then we leave, with plenty of time to spare, for the airport.

The extra time is totally used up driving round and round Heathrow Airport trying to find the Hertz rent-a-car depot. 'You are not paying attention to the map,' huffs HRH.

'I don't have one,' I snap back.

A brief hostile stand-off takes place.

'Well, you should have one,' he insists just to get in the last word. He inherited the must-have-the-last-word gene from his mother, and it's been passed on to, at least, one child in the family. Whereas I come from a family who specialised in the art of inflaming the situation. My family's motto is: 'To solve all problems, pour on petrol, and throw in a lit match.'

'Oh, yes, good,' I reply. 'Well I must get a world map marking all Hertz rent-a-car depots tattooed on my chest. Just so we have one when we need one.'

He says nothing but I know what he's thinking. He's thinking 'Go on then. Do it.'

The children are assuming a remarkably well-behaved stance in the back seat.

But I'm not about to rear children dedicated to indecision. I insist that they pick sides.

'Do you think I should get a tattoo of Hertz rent-a-car depots on my chest?' I ask.

They give me *that* look which says, 'Be a good girl now and take your medication.'

We parents are saved from having to stage a duel on the tarmac at Heathrow when Ms Bright-And-Alert chirps, 'There it is. There's the Hertz sign.' She is pointing to the much-desired destination. It is located two overpasses and one road system back to our left.

It takes another half an hour to turn the car in the opposite direction. Heathrow Airport, like other airports around the world, caters with extraordinary efficiency to motorists who know where they are going. Those in doubt just have to keep driving until they run out of petrol. We thought we'd have to telephone the Hertz folk and say: 'We've returned the car. It's at the airport. Somewhere.' But we were saved.

With only about twenty minutes to the flight we arrive with nearly explosive baggage at the airline check-in counter. It is closed. We rant. We rave. We have, after all, an abundance of aggressive hormones already in play. And they are very effective. We get attention and we get our seats. They have to offload four passengers!

Finally the 747 taxis down a runway at Heathrow. We are heading for home. We sit for the next twenty-four hours like jellied amoebas. Listless. Lifeless. Spent. I watch that little line on the airline computer edge its way slowly back to the great southern land. The words, 'We're goin' home,' never, ever sounded so good.

EUROPEAN EPILOGUE or Please Remind Me Why We Did This Again!

When it comes to travelling the world with the family the first question you have to ask is: 'Why do it?'

Who would inflict upon themselves the economic trauma and emotional torture of collecting together the likes of one irritable spouse, various grumbling children and half a kilogram of motion sickness tablets and travel halfway around the world to visit all of the Great McDonald's of Europe? Who would do it? Me, of course, but I had my reasons. Creating memories for the children was one of them.

Those childhood memories, sealed with crystal clarity in those back pockets of our brains, often recall an event which flung us out of the monotonous grey familiarity of our everyday lives into another dimension — the seaside holiday, the school concert, the birthday. So, for the children, and for our middle-aged selves, we headed out on the Grand Tour of Europe. And they'll have memories all right, but not necessarily those I had in mind. Here are some.

Communication breakdown
Neither of them will forget the Waterford Crystal Factory in Ireland. We, the parents, were so pleased. We had raved about the Waterford Crystal Factory for some time, and the children showed an almost discernible enthusiasm for this tour.

We arrived. They sat in the car. Finally one complained, 'Is this it? The Waterford Crystal Factory? We thought you said a Water Pistol Factory!' But they liked it.

Souvenir addicts unite
I had ideas about the historical value of the European adventure. We visited the Roman baths at Bath, for instance. 'What do you think?' I ask. 'It's a heap of stones,' replies the nine-year-old. 'But they are old. They are Roman Stones,' I gasp. 'Are they older than our stones in Australia?' 'No,' I reply. 'So,' she insists. 'Why are we looking at them?'

It's hard to relate the impact of the Roman Empire on civilisation to the back of a nine-year-old child bolting towards the souvenir shop.

Being bored to semi-consciousness by the 'heap of stones' didn't stop Miss Spending-Money-Is-My-Middle-Name from wanting to buy twenty-five replica Roman coins in the souvenir shop. As a result I developed a policy concerning souvenirs. 'You must look at the real thing before buying a souvenir.'

Remember, 'Rome wasn't built in a day,' but they can churn out thousands of tacky souvenirs every few seconds.

I've got the whole world in my head
I thought the children might gain some geographical insights from the Grand Tour of Europe. Alas, not. The younger tourer remained slumped in the back seat of the hire car most of the time groaning, 'I feel s-iiiiiiick,' (she suffers from motion sickness) and moaning, 'Are we there yet?' every five minutes while the elder tourer sat with the CD plugs in his ears, and his nose in a rock and roll magazine. I had to whack him on the knee and hand

signal, 'Look out the window. Interesting geographical feature.' He would then look up for two seconds, nod that he had seen the abbey ruins, Roman aquaduct or windmill and return to his magazine.

> Often their father was driving the wrong way down a one-way street in peak hour traffic.

The rest of the time in the car they spent arguing over who had rights to the armrest, often while their father was driving the wrong way down a one-way street in peak hour traffic in, say, Eindhoven. The country we parents enjoyed the most was Luxembourg. They both slept though Luxembourg.

But they have memories. The bogs in Ireland. The Irish donkeys. At one B&B our daughter sat on a fence playing her tin flute to the donkey for hours. Unlike her family, he didn't complain.

They'll also remember the Metro in Paris. The London buses. The sheep in Devon. We couldn't work out how the sheep stayed on the steep slopes. We reckoned the farmer had to go out each morning, pick up the sheep that had rolled down the hill overnight and put them back again.

But more than anything else, they know that despite humanity's efforts to wound and scar this weary earth, it is still a stunningly beautiful place.

FIVE

JAPAN

The Land Where They Can't Say 'No'

To view an eastern culture is, for most travellers from the West, a view through a very small window. If you cannot read, hear or in any way converse in the language, then it is much harder to explore the heart of the culture. Information comes to you filtered through your own language and hence your own culture. And some of the major differences and eccentricities can be lost.

Take Japan, for instance. It took me some time to discover that there is no word in polite use for 'No' in the Japanese language. The Japanese are far too well-mannered to say 'No' outright in conversation. The negative must therefore be circumvented, worked around, or approached along an indirect path.

I was flabbergasted. I could not imagine being a mother in a land where you can't say 'No'.

'Can I have a Coke?'

'It would be inappropriate for you to consume a Coke as you request at the present moment.'

Motherhood must be a nightmare of stumbling over convoluted sentences. But it explains, in part, why you might see unrestrained glee in the eyes of Japanese children dropping, say, dumplings from a great height into their soup at a restaurant. Obviously, by the time the parents get around to saying, 'Kindly desist from the practice of dropping dumplings into your soup,' the kids have already done it three times!

But there is one positive factor working in a parent's favour. While it is impolite in Japan to say 'No' directly, it is even more impolite to ask, 'Why?' straight out. Thus, when a child in Japan is told it is an inappropriate time to have a Coke, they cannot whine, 'Why?' They would be forced to say: 'Could you kindly explain the reason behind a Coke being inappropriate at this interlude?' Or something to that effect. This is good news for parents. By the time the kid has spat out that sentence, McDonald's would be miles back!

And thus another small window opened for me into the culture. But this revelation only reinforced the vision of Japan as an enigma. Here, on the one hand, was an insight into the convoluted nature of the language used in a polite society, yet Japanese shrines, temples, gardens, flower arrangements, and ceramic work are composed with a poetry of simplicity. A complexity of words clutter a land where simple beauty is art.

THE BONSAI BRA

I'm in Yokohama on business. I'm travelling light. I take with me: one husband, no children, four credit cards, and a big grin. The grin is essential. Being unable to use my mouth for the purpose of communicating with locals, I have to keep it occupied doing other things.

My business is to write fascinating articles about Japan. HRH's business is to survive a work trip spent entirely in buildings fitted wall to wall with smoking co-workers and heated to 28°C. He is trying to remain dignified in a work enviroment which is a cross between a Turkish bath and a volcano.

I wander the city alone. I feel very foreign and very tall. I'm nearly 1.7 metres tall, though I'm losing ground in Australia. The younger generation of Australians is whipping past me so quickly, sometimes I think I'm shrinking. But here, in Yokohama, I'm tall.

The current generation of teenagers in Japan is certainly growing taller. You bump into tall, thin and very polite boys 1.8 metres and over in Japan every day. But their parents are, by our standards, short. As for their grandparents, they are like miniature dolls. I can stand in a department store lift in Japan and feel like Michael Jordan.

In Japan — the land where women have such fine and delicate features, they shame the beauty of the cherry blossom — I thought

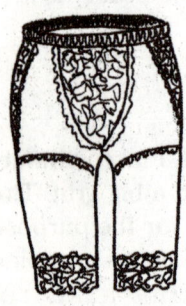

Trousseauu from the Proportion Make collection

I would, with my height and wholesomeness, feel like a sumo wrestler with a handbag. But I don't, not entirely, and there is a reason.

The first inkling I receive that Japanese women are not all perfectly proportioned China dolls comes in the form of a mail order brochure. I am looking at the bust, waist and hip measurement chart when I am struck with a lightning flash realisation that each and every one of these figures from size 7–19 is pear-shaped.

I am talking fine and delicate pears. I'm a size 14 in Australia. I'm a 19 or XLL in Japan. But on this chart every hip measurement is five centimetres larger than the bust.

And this difference has created a sense of longing in Japanese women, especially young girls, that genetics cannot fulfil. Japanese women want a bustline — a cleavage. And they go to extraordinary lengths to acquire that extra bounce.

The tragic irony of this situation hit me with the force of a typhoon. In Australia, girls are constantly trying to slim down to the waif-like proportions of Japanese girls. While in Japan girls are trying desperately, ever so desperately, to beef up. In the right places, of course.

I ask two Japanese girls to tell me who represents the ideal of womanhood for Japanese women? Naomi Campbell, they answer in unison. Pitiful, isn't it? Women the world over burden themselves with these impossible goals. How can Japanese girls ever look like a 1.8 metre Afro-American beanpole with a bustline?

They try. In Japan, for example, there is no such thing as an unpadded bra. The lingerie department is full of pink bras, lemon bras, aqua bras. Rack after rack of twin-padded pastel patty pans. They are mostly size A bras. From the perspective of an Aussie gal, these are bonsai bras!

I decide to test drive a Japanese bra. I slip into a cubicle and out again in a hurry. I had not taken my shoes off. I take them off, bow and return. I must tell you if I was trying on cubicles, I'd want one two sizes bigger. Bra-wise, Wow! In Japan I'm 'Dorry Parton!' Normally a 34B, I'm a 75D here. Add the padding, and if I stood in the street they'd think I was a bus shelter!

Bras are not the only apparel items to reshape the figure. Panties are designed to lift bottoms. Lift and separate. Pantihose too. Pantihose names include: GOOD UP, SHOCK UP and MODEL UP. One pantihose brand was called 'HIP MAKING'. They want hips, in the right place. We've got hips to spare in Australia. It's a pity we can't export hips, improve our deficit and everyone would be happy including the Prime Minister.

More drastic body-shaping measures include: BUST PANIC, a bust-enlarging cream; an electric padded bra which vibrates a girl to cleavage heaven; twin-suction cups with a pump; rubber body-sauna garments which reshape the body using 'focused perspiration'; and cosmetic surgery procedures called BUST UP and A SWELL AND SLACK.

✈ ✈ ✈ ✈ ✈

In the serenity of a Japanese garden near my hotel, I take time out to think.

> Nature reflects wisdom
> The cherry blossom blooms
> But it does not try to be
> A lotus flower.

THE LAND OF THE VIBRATING CHAIR

The next day we catch a train from Yokohama to Tokyo in peak hour. I'm doing this purely for the educational experience, and not for the joy of being canned alive with people I don't know!

It is difficult for Australians to wrap their minds around the scale of Japan. There are 124 million people in Japan, which sounds quite a few, really. Japan's land base is roughly half the size of New South Wales. That sounds okay except only three per cent of the land is available for housing, the rest being dedicated to roads, mountains and farms. This means 124 million people live in one-sixth the area of Tasmania. That's the size of a golf course in Australia, surely.

Yet, you only feel overwhelmed by vast numbers of people at certain times, in certain places. Yokohama station at peak hour is one such place. Stepping into the vast underground caverns of Yokohama station is like stumbling on to the set of *Earthquake*. There are people charging in every direction in a state of absolute panic. God help them if they ever have an earthquake at Yokohama station. No one will notice.

HRH and I fight our way to the platform and wait in line for the Tokyo train. (HRH, His Royal Hairiness, has a full but trim Father Christmas-style beard which often made the Japanese men around him look like boys of sixty!)

The train arrives and it is full. Packed. Bursting along its aluminium seams. This makes no difference. The doors open. The crowd surges forward and we are carried with it. We are squeezed into that carriage like the contents of a tube of toothpaste.

Fortunately, our heads are above the crowd so we can breathe. Just. But I can't move my arms, and it is hot, hellishly hot. The train is heated as well. I knew if I fainted I wouldn't fall — half the business men around us are sound asleep, standing. But I want to get my coat off. I manage to extract one arm from the crush. HRH holds the cuff, with his teeth I think, and I worm my way out of the jacket. It is like playing Strip Twister in a packed lift. Try it some time.

When the forty-five minute trip is up, I fall out of the train on to the platform and inhale for the next ten minutes. We have been breathing solid low level sweat for the last half hour. Lots of Japanese workers do this trip every day, twice a day. Peak hour in Japan is from 8 a.m. to 10 a.m., and 8 p.m. to 10 p.m. They must arrive at the office pressed flat like a flower. It probably takes them several hours each morning just to pop back into shape.

I decided that if Churchill described Russia as 'a riddle wrapped in a mystery inside an enigma' then Japan could be described as 'a riddle wrapped in cellophane paper with a little gold sticker inside a floral wrap'. For the Japanese are batty about packaging. I find this totally ironic.

On the one hand, people are shunted about the place as if part of the live sheep trade from Australia. On the other hand, a slice of chocolate cake is treated as if it were a member of the Imperial family. It is lovingly cut and packaged in so many layers of paper art, you spend much more time unwrapping it than eating it. Even a Teriyaki McBurger and takeaway Coke at McDonald's come inside cellophane wraps inside a carry bag.

> *A slice of chocolate cake is treated as if it were a member of the Imperial Family.*

So the average officeworker in Japan works long hours and spends a lot of time unwrapping their lunch, but they do have — compared to us — a high disposable income. With only comparatively low tax and food prices roughly the same as ours, they can buy a lot of stuff. And they do.

I may feel foreign in Japan, but I also feel comfortable. Quite comfortable. It takes me time to work out why. Japan is predominantly a middle-class society. It reminds me of my cosy little middle-class suburb in Melbourne multiplied by lots and lots of people who like to buy gismos. It's yuppie world. It's just like home.

I see so many Louis Vuitton bags in Japan I begin to suspect they are giving them away with the Teriyaki McBurgers in a cellophane wrap. Everyone seems to have a mobile phone, but they are so small — just a bit bigger than a cigarette lighter — it looks like people are walking around with one of their thumbs in their ear, talking to their little finger. You can buy an electric anything. Toilet Seat. No worries. It sprays. It blow dries. It probably plays the Last Post and all. Electric chair. No problems. But this is a massage chair. I try it. It thuds. It wallops. It massages down my back. Satisfaction guaranteed. With this chair, you could have an extramarital affair without the inconvenience of having to leave the comfort of your own lounge-room.

But there is one problem. What does a committed Japanese consumer do with the old gismo when the next model hits the shops? They chuck it. Dump it in the rubbish, or *gommi* pile. Any smart young Australian setting up house in Japan doesn't buy appliances. They hit the *gommi* piles around the blocks of flats picking up as-new TVs, CD players, bicycles. Whatever. We leave the big department stores of Tokyo feeling, if anything, a little sad.

So geared are the young Japanese to consumption, very soon, perhaps, we will find their ancient culture — that riddle wrapped in cellophane — dumped on the *gommi* pile.

✈ ✈ ✈ ✈ ✈

But there are more cultural landmines waiting to explode in our faces on the streets of Tokyo. Japan is a land of many inconsistencies built on a contradiction. In this technically proficient and highly organised society, which can produce a ten-storey indoor ski slope with snow, or a working model of a car as big as a grain of rice, there are no addresses — as we know them. No street names, or very few. No house numbers like ours, just area names. And confusion.

Even if you can find your way to the designated area given in an address, the building number is no help. Buildings aren't numbered numerically. They are numbered in chronological order based on when they were built. No. 543 might be next door to No. 2.

Moreover, a map of inner Tokyo is a blank grid with a few building names. Fortunately, we find people in the street are very happy to help with directions. I think it's because they know what it's like to be lost — from experience.

You often see people walking in well-formed groups behind a flag-carrying leader in many cities in Japan. I suspect it's just office workers being led home from work! We join one group by default and we are led to a railway station. Thank God. We catch the Sardine Special back to Yokohama and the spacious surrounds of our small hotel room.

IN JAPAN, GIRLS JUST WANT TO HAVE FUN

Back in my hotel room, I ponder the curiosity that is Japan. In this land, the breeding ground of robotic technology and electrical wizardry, people are employed to do jobs which are performed by gadgets elsewhere. In Australia, the job of guarding a hole in the road would be performed by a flashing yellow light. In Japan, more often than not, two uniformed men with whistles, wearing white gloves and carrying a flashing red baton will guard that hole day and night.

In a culture where people are so polite they bow talking on the telephone, where leather-jacket-wearing bikies will profusely apologise if they bump into you in the street, and where women are too polite to use a toilet without a background flushing noise (to save water there are speakers which broadcast a flushing sound installed in public toilets), smokers line you up between the eyes and blow smoke in your face. That is an exaggeration but in Japan smokers rule. 'This is a non-smoking flight' means, according to my experience, no smoking during this announcement.

I also discover that a traditional wedding in Japan is not very traditional at all. I stand watching a wedding in the lobby of our five-star hotel in Yokohama. This lobby is the essence of kitsch overkill. Marble steps rise to a mezzanine floor sweeping above a two-storey waterfall, backlit to create a simulated fire effect. With the public announcement, 'Ladies and Gentleman, I introduce Mr and Mrs Morimoto,' the couple, dressed from head to toe in formal white bridal garb, glide down the staircase as the orchestra plays, and bubbles billow from the bottom of the marble steps. Frankly, I have a tear in my eye until I am told, 'It's acting. They're hotel employees. They stage this wedding five times a day on Sunday to sell the wedding package.' And hard work it is too.

There has been a revolution taking place in Japan over the last ten years. A quiet revolution. With the introduction of the Equal Employment Opportunity Law in 1986, women gained the right to equal pay with men. Not that the young working girls spend all their money wisely. I saw girls in platform shoes that were so high they could have bungy jumped off them. But social change is afoot.

Traditionally, in Japan, women rule the home. Wives take the pay packet and give him back pocket money only. So definite is the wives' home rule, they even have terms for husbands who get in the way. They are called *gokiburi teisha*; cockroach husbands. What could be more annoying in the kitchen than a cockroach?

Tradition dictates that when a girl marries she will resign from her job, take up home duties and focus on the family. But times have changed. Until 1986, Japanese girls had little spending power and therefore little choice. In 1985 only thirty per cent of Japanese girls in their twenties remained unmarried. In 1995, (shock! *sa, taihen-da*! horror!) fifty per cent of girls in their twenties remained unmarried.

The young girls I speak to about marriage just shake their heads and say: 'No. No. No. Not yet. Later.'

But what does this mean? This means roughly a thirty per cent drop in the number of marriages in ten years. And in Japan marriage is big business. Brides don't wear just one bridal dress. Often they wear three: the full Princess Di regalia for the ceremony; then, typically, an over-the-top Barbara Cartland meets Scarlet O'Hara electric pink tulle number for the reception; and a white kimono for the Shinto blessing. These are not exactly outfits a girl will get to wear again.

Then there are the presents for the guests. At a middle-class wedding, guests may be given a catalogue and they may pick, perhaps, a VCR for their efforts. Such a wedding could cost A$80 000. On a good day. On a really good day, parents might be coughing up A$100 000.

It's not surprising that the wedding venues are totting for custom. Their customers, tragically, are staying single in droves.

There is little talk of feminism in Japan. But in the land of the rising sun, girls are rebelling. Politely.

I watch the pretend Mrs Morimoto glide down the steps and into the hotel foyer, and I feel like yelling, 'Go girl,' for she is, despite appearances, a working girl — a member of the sisterhood and a part of the revolution.

SIX

DESPERATELY SEEKING AMERICA

I utter the word 'Disneyland' and call for volunteers. Ms Stormtrooper jumps around the kitchen in a frenzy of enthusiasm insisting that we pack immediately and leave the next day for America. Mr Intense Teenager says he is too busy with his rock band. He'll stay at school. Ms Stormtrooper looks at him as if he is three drums short of a full kit. HRH says he'll go if he can plan the itinerary, and if the itinerary that he plans is then obeyed.

It is agreed. We'll do a skyscraper tour of the United States of America: LA, San Francisco, New York, and Washington. Miss I've-Always-Wanted-To-Be-An-Only-Child will travel with us. We will fly between cities, and the itinerary will be obeyed. Repeat. The itinerary will be obeyed.

YOU SAY 'HAVE NICE DAY'; WE SAY 'BUGGER OFF'

One of the great shocks for Australians arriving in America is the discovery that we are *not* American. The problem is, back in Australia, we are bombarded daily to the point of saturation by the gargantuan multi-media ferocity of the United States of America. So, tucked away in our own little corner of the Pacific Ocean, we begin to believe we are the 51st state of America.

This is only confirmed by what we see around us: McDonald's, Pizza Hut, baseball caps, sneakers, rap music, the Planet Hollywoods, the Hard Rock Cafes, Las Vegas-style casinos, and cellulite everywhere! It's not only how we dress and what we eat that makes us think we are Yankee Doodle Dandies downunder, it is also what we hear in everyday speech. Every hour of every day we hear Americanisms slipping into common use.

As if the early wartime invasions of 'okay', 'schmozzle', 'double whammy' and 'hunky-dory' weren't enough, now we hear Aussie kids on the street exclaiming a Homer Simpson 'D'Oh' or an Eddie Murphyesque 'Yoh!'. Australians seem to be preoccupied with being 'awesome' or 'cool'; we talk about 'dudes' and 'nerds' and have enthusiastically embraced the concept of 'doing lunch'. And we often hear terms thrown around like: 'It's time to kick some butt' or 'He's the big honcho' or 'We had the full enchilada.' And we wonder from time to time whatever happened to the good old Aussie lingo or fair dinkum Strine. It must have kicked the bucket or carked it.

We continue to think we are American until we do one thing. Visit America. Then we are hit in the face with the harsh glare of reality and we realise we are not American. We are not even part-time Yanks, thanks. We are neither ocker Eddie Murphies or fair dinkum Bart Simpsons.

Sure, we borrow words and phrases from America. Language is, after all, the most democratic process on earth. We vote every day for our preferred language with our mouths.

If we in Australia start saying 'have a nice day' instead of the more casual Aussie 'see ya!' or the laconic 'bugger off' (I mean laconic in the sense that 'bugger off' can constitute quite a warm and friendly farewell in Australia much in the same way as 'you old bastard' can be a term of endearment), if we replace 'g'day mate' with 'yoh! my man', or 'nice bum' with 'great buns' then it is because we choose to do so. No one is making us speak American. There are no vocabulary police.

But even if we choose to use these Americanisms we are still not American. I made this discovery on arriving in the States when I found America to be, in many ways, more foreign, more bizarre, more indecipherable than Europe or Japan.

It was in Los Angeles that I discovered I was not American. I found myself separated from Americans by a language barrier so vast and so broad that often we could not reach each other across it. We were, amazingly, separated by a common language.

The first problem was the accent. Americans didn't understand me. Often. How could they not understand me? I cut my teeth on American TV series — 'Jungle Jim', 'The Texas Rangers', 'My Three Sons', 'Father Knows Best'; I lived for 'Gunsmoke', 'Rifleman' and 'The Cisco Kid'. I dedicated my life to becoming a Mouseketeer. I grew up with 'The Brady Bunch'. I could have dated Greg. I've even watched reruns of reruns of 'Gilligan's Island'. How could they not understand me? I can speak American. Can't I? Well, yes and no.

I knew I had an accent of sorts. Australians tend to take all of those rounded English vowels and flatten them down with a hammer. But the British can understand us, and our English-speaking Dutch relatives had no trouble.

In America, I was not understood. I asked if I could wash my hands in the 'basin'. That left one American with a look on their face that suggested they were thinking: 'These Aussies are a little off the planet.' To the American ear, I was asking if I could wash my hands in a 'bison'. A buffalo!

Some Aussie friends were down South trying to buy a tent from the classified advertisements in a local newspaper. They would ring up and ask about the 'tent' advertised, and receive bemused and confused replies. Eventually, by describing the item as a little canvas house for camping, one Southerner latched on to what the Aussie was on about, namely: 'Yo'all mean a tay-ent.'

'Yeah.'

Not only do we Aussies hammer syllables flat, we tend to run them all together. I heard a great example of this during a travel tales segment on talk-back radio. Some Australians caught a taxi from the airport to their hotel in Chicago, say, I can't remember. On the way they asked the driver, 'How much is a local phone call?' They asked five times. And five times there was no reply. Finally, our intrepid Aussies, having paid for the fare, dared to ask, 'Why won't you tell us the price of a local phone call?' The cabbie just pushed his cap to the back of his head and asked, 'What's a larkle farkle?' A LARKLE FARKLE! You shouldn't leave home without one.

Accent aside, there are many, many factors contributing to this gulf of confusion caused by a common language. There is the quite significant problem associated with the fact that a number of words and phrases in common use have different meanings in each culture.

If an American is 'pissed' they are angry. If an Australian is 'pissed' they are drunk. Of course, an Australian can get well and truly 'pissed off' — the Aussie angry — especially if no one understands what they are talking about. Americans 'root' for their team. In Australia the term 'root' can be used as a blunt four-letter word, so that 'rooting for a team' downunder would be quite exhausting and little short of an orgy.

Australians 'barrack' for their teams. But most Americans have never heard of the term 'barrack'. 'In Ost-rail-ee-a you bar-ack for your team?' The word leaves the American mouth as an elongated 'bark'. Americans must think, 'They don't whoop 'n' holler in Ost-rail-ee-a, they obviously "Woof."'

> *If an American is 'pissed' they are angry. If an Australian is 'pissed' they are drunk.*

Another factor contributing to this minefield of misunderstanding spread between the two cultures is caused by the general ignorance or total apathy concerning Australia on the part of many Americans. As far as I could work out, quite a few Americans don't seem to know Australia exists, or they don't care. Why should they? Australia has about as much impact on the culture of America as a butterfly being sucked into the engines of a jumbo jet.

When I first visited America some years ago, one shop assistant on hearing I was from Australia asked, 'Is that where all the children are starving?' I claimed not. I just thought some well-meaning American might overhear and attempt to fly in emergency drops of pastrami on rye, or buckets of ketchup.

One waiter thought Australia was near Germany. This was post-*Crocodile Dundee*, I assure you. But Australia is often confused with Austria, for obvious reasons. I dare say that waiter is still wondering why Crocodile Dundee wasn't wearing little leather shorts, a Tyrolean hat and singing 'Edel Weis' in the swamp.

Thanks to advertisements for Foster's Lager, a current image of Australians held by some Americans today makes Crocodile

Dundee look like an intellectual. In one ad an Aussie bloke throws a boomerang at the TV set with the accompanying words, 'Australian for remote control. Foster's, Australian for beer.' Another ad shows an Aussie bloke and, I have to use the term, sheila, having an arm wrestle followed by the words, 'Australian for marriage counselling.' And yet another ad shows a two-kilogram steak thrown on to a barbie with a sprig of parsley on top captioned, 'Australian for side salad.'

I can't say that Americans think we Aussies are awesome, but the ones that I met seemed to think we were quite lovable and quaint, like koo-ell-ar bears, and surprisingly intelligent for a race who spends their time throwing boomerangs at television sets.

If so often Australians and Americans cannot reach each other across the barrier of a 'common' language, how different must our cultures be? Australians are not American. And more than anything else, I wish in this section to describe, celebrate, marvel and fearlessly record some of those many things American, Aussies aren't.

DON'T SHOOT! I'M A TOURIST

There are many things travellers in America worry about. 'Will I ever get to the end of this queue?' is a common worry. The British, some say, have made a hobby out of queuing. America, on the other hand, has turned queuing into a science. Nowhere else in the world are there more chrome poles with interlocking nylon belts turning queues into giant mazes which can only be solved by carefully following the person in front of you for such a length of time you begin to feel you have turned into their pet.

I tell you one thing, if the end of the world is really nigh, then on Judgement Day I hope the queues are organised by Americans. Then it would be done in an orderly fashion and it would save us having to stand around an entire eternity waiting to be processed.

Other things travellers worry about in America include: buying a pair of ornamental cow horns for the lounge-room wall (it seemed like a good idea at the time), overdosing on ketchup, developing an excessive fondness for dropping a dollop of jelly — alias jam — in the middle of almost anything fried, and being overcome by an urge to discuss your sex life openly on the 'Oprah Winfrey Show'.

But what travellers worry about most in America is living to tell the tale or, at least, show the folks back home the video of the trip. I blame television. Statistics show that the average television viewer will see more people shot or blown up or otherwise disposed of on TV each year than inhabit the entire East Coast of America. Or, if you happen to be watching any of the popular disaster movies, you can see the entire population of the East Coast of America wiped out in one film.

The novice traveller in America can hardly believe that they can travel along a freeway without incident, without police cars flying over the top of them, without long-haul trucks trying to squash them into the guard rails, without Thelma and Louise blinding them with a trail of dust.

The novice traveller can hardly believe they may occupy a high-rise hotel room without Bruce Willis smashing in through a window on a rope, or stand in front of the Empire State Building without World War III breaking out overhead, or go anywhere in America without the arrival of an unscheduled tornado, volcano or earthquake.

Unfortunately, on arrival in this country this unsafe vision of America is only reinforced in the mind of the tourist by certain little cultural artefacts such as bumper stickers. Here are a few:

- Driver Carries Only $20.00 In Ammunition
- Gun Control Means Using Both Hands
- I Still Miss My 'X' But My Aim Is Improving.

A sign in the subway might strike fear into the heart of a tourist. Here's one from the San Francisco Metro:

> Information gladly given but safety requires avoiding unnecessary conversation.

A newspaper report might start the alarm bells ringing in the mind of the tourist. Here's one I read in *Entertainment Weekly*:

> Rapper Snoop Doggy Dog is leaving his current label, Death Row Records, because he fears for his life.

And what was his new label choice? Solitary Confinement. He should feel safe there!

Or it might just be a simple ad in a local catalogue that makes the tourist feel uncomfortable. Very uncomfortable. Here's one I found in the High Street Emporium Catalogue in LA:

'Don't drive without Safe-T Man as your bodyguard. Designed as a visual deterrent, Safe-T Man is a life-size, simulated male that appears to be 180 lbs and 6 feet tall, to give others the impression that you are protected by a male guardian while at home alone or driving your car.

'This unique security device looks incredibly real with a positionable latex head and hands, air-brushed facial highlights, and salt-and-pepper hair. Made of the highest quality, inflatable PVC, he weighs just 7 lbs and can be dressed according to your own personal style. When not keeping vigil over your well-being, deflate, store and transport him inconspicuously in the optional tote bag. Comes with a repair patch.'

A repair patch! My God, you can wear him out.

To allay the fears of the traveller, I feel I should introduce a few statistics. In a good year there are about 25 000 homicides in America. This is no statistic to celebrate. It is, per head of population, roughly five times that experienced in Australia.

But homicide is not the main slayer of Americans. Obesity is the big killer. When the 'Shape Up America' campaign was launched in America a few years ago statistics were released which suggested that obesity contributed to the deaths annually of 300 000 Americans. This is something tourists should worry about. If you apply

Misadventure land, perhaps!

basic common sense to travelling around America — in other words, you do not get out of the subway in the wrong part of town at night, drunk and carrying an open wallet — then you are unlikely to meet anyone intent on turning you into a homicide statistic.

But in everyday touring of everyday places you do see quite a few Americans carrying quite a bit of excess baggage. Now 300 000 Americans have to reach the deceased state by the end of the year. One of them standing in front of you in a queue could easily have the heart attack, fall on you and take you out with them.

Yep, obesity. That's what you've got to worry about in America. So if you see the person in front of you starting to wobble in a queue — run for your life.

THE STARS AT NIGHT Have No Cellulite Deep in the Heart of LA

Los Angeles is the city where Hollywood meets the rest of the world, where fantasy meets reality, and where people, sometimes, can't tell the difference.

We fly into LA International Airport 'where the big jet engines run'. Sorry, I can't help bursting into song whenever I go to America. LA Airport is under reconstruction. We are talking major disaster movie crossed with the LA marathon in leisure suits. People running everywhere. It's wall-to-wall bedlam. I expect Charlton Heston to pop out of the lift and save me by leading me to my luggage. Or perhaps they could send in a crack team of paratroopers to airlift me to safety. This is not so far-fetched. I found a list of emergency contacts with a number for Military Airlift Command in the women's toilets. You can have faith in a country where a girl could order an invasion of Iraq while powdering her nose.

Leaving the airport we pass a domed restaurant on legs which is straight out of 'The Jetsons'. We're in sunny California and it's raining. Real rain. Wait a minute. This is LA. I look around for the big fan and the rain-maker props. I can't see any. It's real rain all right, hammering on to the tarmac like bullets.

We board a bus and head into LA proper. 'LA is a freeway' according to one song. People drive everywhere in LA. Even to their letterboxes, I suspect. So the freeways are big. Some of them are twelve lanes wide and stacked three high. I begin to believe it would be possible to conceive and give birth on an LA freeway before finding the right exit. Of course, you would have to make appropriate adjustments to the driver's seat.

Fortunately, I'm not driving. The driver, however, seems more 'Hollywood here I am' than a Bus Department regular. He points out that we are on the very freeway where they filmed the movie *Speed*. And he's speeding, the fool. It's just the sort of thing you want to hear when you're in the bus from hell and there's not one Keanu Reeves in sight. Fifteen minutes into the journey, Ms I-Get-Car-sick-You-Know lives up to her name and we find ourselves on a speeding bus in the rain with nothing to deal with the emergency other than three scrunched up tissues. We manage, but I begin to believe Keanu Reeves had an easy time on that bus.

The truth is I worry about being in LA. Courtesy of Hollywood we see so many gallons of designer blood splattered on corpses with perfect teeth each night on telly, it's hard to believe LA is a safe place. I tell myself get a grip. You are on a tourist bus on the way to Disneyland. What could happen? Nothing. Then I find out that the day before a tourist bus was shot at five kilometres from Disneyland. No one was killed but from then on everyone on the street began to look like Michael Douglas in *Falling Down*.

We arrive safely at the Disneyland Hotel. No bullet holes. No Michael Douglas. But I see a guy behind a bar straight out of 'Friends' and a woman customer is from the 'Drew Carey Show'. I swear.

Mickey Mouse is everywhere. There are Mickey Mouse hedges and Mickey Mouse brass statues in the foyer. You get Mickey Mouse ice blocks in your drink, Mickey Mouse soap in the bathroom, Mickey Mouse pancakes, Mickey Mouse-shaped toast. This is an amazing hotel: 1638 guest rooms. You need a map to find your room. But I was disappointed that we didn't have a Mickey Mouse-shaped bed or a shower cap with Mickey Mouse ears. Next time.

So Disneyland here we come! We have one child and one day to do the lot. And it is raining cats and dogs. Wait a minute, this is LA. It's probably raining hairstylists and breast implants. We have the good fortune to arrive in sunny California during the weather event of the century (flooding, mud slides, etc). We're in Disneyland looking for Mickey Mouse. At this stage, he'd have to look like a drowned rat. It is so wet down Main Street I would not have been surprised if Humphrey Bogart staggered past towing the *African Queen*. If, on the other hand, Gene Kelly had come prancing past 'singing in the rain' I would have whacked him on the ear with my umbrella. I wasn't very happy about the rain. We bought our Mickey Mouse umbrellas at the gate and sloshed in.

On the plus side, when you are wading through water fifteen centimetres deep, there are no queues. You can walk straight on to a ride! On the down side, the rollercoasters are half full of water. We do the Matterhorn ride in little half-filled bath tubs. I start looking for Kevin Costner. We must have strayed on to the *Waterworld* set by mistake.

When the rain lifts, instant crowds return. We have to queue for rides; fifty minutes for some. I expect the sign which tells you how long you've got to wait in the queue for the Indiana Jones ride to say 'Not in Your Lifetime'. But it is worth the wait. The ride turns out to be so fantastic, the robotics so stunningly real, I didn't think I'd been on a theme park ride at all. I thought I'd just had an affair with Harrison Ford. True.

The quintessential Disneyland ride is the submarine. You queue to get into an artificial submarine, to go into an artificial lake, to look at artificial fish. That's fantasy, American style.

Back in reality, I can no longer avoid buying a souvenir. There are souvenirs everywhere for every ride and every restaurant. You go to the toilet, you think you should buy a souvenir. There are even Mickey Mouse dollar bills. Don't laugh. The Mickey dollar is currently worth more than the Aussie dollar.

Sloshing through Fantasyland in the rain to catch the Monorail back to the hotel, suddenly I realise what is going on. Everyone is blaming El Nino. Rubbish! Or, if you prefer, trash! We've been caught up in something far more sinister and far more diabolical. This is the *Revenge of Fantasia*. We have arrived at Disneyland the day the buckets are winning.

WHO YA GONNA CALL?

I'm intrigued with American money. Each note, each dime has 'In God We Trust' written on it. When fronted with yet another bill plus tax I feel like saying: 'Don't look at me. God's paying.' I think someone should test this trust.

Needless to say Americans take religion seriously and California is a very religious state. I counted seventy-nine separate Christian religions alone in the LA phone book. It's an LA thing. Designer religion.

I love the names. Coming from a culture where the most flamboyant name of a church might be Our Lady of Mercy or St John of God, some of the LA congregation names were, by comparison, a riot: Creation Good News Church of God, Centre of Enlightenment, Sweet Mystery of Life Services, and God's House of Deliverance (I don't think this congregation had anything to do with the film, but it would be very spooky if they started playing banjos in the church!).

My favourite was the church called Holy Ghost Repair Service Inc. It sounds so LA. If you are in a spiritual crisis in Los Angeles, 'Who ya gonna call?' Holy Ghost Busters, I guess.

But this is LA, liposuction capital of the world, where cellulite is a sin and coveting thy neighbour's wife is a popular sport. I'm fascinated by a magazine ad for Body Sculpture cream. This fat reduction cream claims users lose an average 2.1 inches from each thigh in only two weeks. This cream has no drugs, just natural active ingredients. What are these miracle natural ingredients? Dynamite? I turn to the next page in the magazine to find myself confronted by a double-page advertisement for Prozac. Well, no wonder the women of LA — and other parts of America might I add — are depressed. They're still waiting for the Body Sculpture cream from the previous page to work.

Still, LA would have to be one of the few places on earth where you can firm your body and shore up your soul at the same time. Yes, with only a few sessions of Gospel Aerobics you will end up with the sort of body you can be proud to take to heaven. What next? Well, one of two things can happen here. Either we'll soon see the St Matthew Work-Out tapes on the video shop shelves or some of the good folk of LA will find a way to start praying to St Silicon.

THIS IS THE DAWNING OF THE MIDDLE AGE OF AQUARIUS

We fly to San Francisco. Every day this crowded city turns itself into a true-life opera set in impossibly steep hills, which, to add to the drama, are perched precariously over the San Andreas Fault. But perhaps it is this threat to its own permanence which gives San Francisco its vigour. Earthquake advice in the phone book includes: 'Don't expect official help for several days and have a kit ready for DIY operations.' Face lifts? Maybe.

For everyone — every ethnic group, every city type or average suburbanite, every deadbeat and every weirdo in every extreme — is out there daily on the streets of San Francisco. Co-existing. The street theatre of San Francisco is so vibrant it seems doubly larger than life, and the setting itself is so picturesque that a jolting uphill and jangling downhill cable car ride from the city centre to Fisherman's Wharf could, due to the number of photo opportunities, wear out a standard busload of camera-toting Japanese tourists. Us too! And we are trying to be moderate.

This is the city which gave the world Janis Joplin, hippies, the Summer of Love, the horror of Alcatraz, the glory of gay pride and the concept of medicinal cannabis. (Sufferers can get together daily at the Cannabis Buyers Club and smoke their ailments away. Cannabis may not actually cure your complaint, but it sure as hell stops you worrying about it.) And San Francisco gave the world the very practical concept of Levi 501s. Yet this city is smaller than Adelaide. The current population of San Francisco is 780 000. Unbelievable.

San Francisco is the great big melting pot. But the gas hasn't been turned on yet. Some ethnic groups cling together — unreconstructed — in small hostile groups. And it's a case of tourist be wary.

If you are white, middle aged and middle class, you can walk down 5th Street. You can walk down 7th Street. But don't go down 6th Street, man, unless 'yo' hankerin' for trouble'. Sixth Street is a bad, bad area. HRH makes this mistake. He is looking for a computer shop and turns innocently into 6th Street. His passage is blocked. He is bumped into, jeered and threatened. He puts his head down, hunches his shoulders and just keeps walking. And this in the middle of the day. If you go down there at night, 'Man, yo' dead!' Maybe. It's like playing Russian roulette with a tourist map. You gotta know your 'hoods, or be able to hum a few bars of Snoop Doggy Dog's latest rap hit.

San Francisco is not all urban angst, it hosts every type of drama — black comedy, soap opera and pantomime. If you want to see the pantomime go to Haight-Ashbury's transvestite shop. It's gorgeous. You'll find lime green feather boas. Purple wigs. Earrings like chandeliers and stretch boa-trimmed bell bottoms for all 6 foot 6 inches of Miss Candy Toes. I love this shop. I've suddenly turned into a 'small' fitting size. I don't want to leave.

Love-ins? It's all still happening in the Haight-Ashbury area. Once the epicentre of the hippy universe, some remnants of psychedelia remain. Tie-dye T-shirts. Love beads. Strange smoking implements. A few hippies. But the Summer of Love was over thirty years ago. The remaining hippies have moved from the age of Aquarius, to the middle age of Aquarius, to the senior citizens of Aquarius in love beads and motorised carts.

> You'll find lime green feather boas. Purple wigs. Earrings like chandeliers and stretch boa-trimmed bell bottoms.

But much has changed in Haight-Ashbury. Now there are punks, goths, drag queens, jocks, the homeless, and cops. We see undercover cops working the street on Ashbury Street. We know they are undercover cops because we see them talking into the top of their windcheaters. Further proof that these bods are police officers, and not psychos on a day out, emerges when the cop in the grey tracksuit whips a pair of handcuffs out of his pocket and waves them in front of a teenage girl with nose studs shouting, 'I told you to put that joint out. I told you. Do you want go in?'

I feel I have fallen back in time into my television set. It is 'The Streets of San Francisco', and I am an unpaid extra. I expect Michael Douglas to pop up any minute wearing a suit with wide lapels.

Take all this drama, and throw in a mixture of Japanese and European tourists, and tourists from middle America, and you have a snapshot of San Francisco. It's a kaleidoscope of values, ethics and attitudes. You can't help but love this confusion.

ESCAPE TO ALCATRAZ

We take a short ride on San Francisco Bay, and there standing in grim isolation, like a dark shadow on the enlightened soul of San Francisco, is Alcatraz. Evil, dark and desolate Alcatraz. An island fortress and a brutal penitentiary. It was first a military base then a federal prison.

It's intriguing to note that the word 'penitentiary' is favoured for penal institutions in America — derived from 'penance'. A penitent is a repenting sinner. Whereas in Australia 'gaol' remains the preferred term, a word connected to law, state and punishment with no religious overtones. The Australian prison system is no more enlightened, but, perhaps, less self-righteous than some parts of the American penal system. The 'eye for an eye, tooth for a tooth' zeal faded decades ago in Australia. There's no capital punishment.

The penance that was done in Alcatraz was done the hard way: Regulation 5; 'You are entitled to food, clothing, shelter and medical attention. Anything else you get is a privilege.' Including a bed.

The word 'slammer' derives from penitentiaries like Alcatraz where the cell door was mechanically designed to slam shut. In Alcatraz, the narrow cells stacked three layers high slammed shut one layer at a time.

It is the sound you hear echoing through every gritty prison movie, those nightmares of violence acted out in real lives. It is the sound of finality, of lost identity, and of despair. We are relieved to catch the two-tiered ferry with a colourful flock of jabbering tourists back to Fisherman's Wharf.

✈ ✈ ✈ ✈ ✈

Walking the streets of this city, we find San Francisco is not so much the city that never sleeps, as the city that doesn't seem to know what it's doing. Or likely to do next.

This is reflected in the legislation. Currently rats are in and smokers are out. Legislators have recently banned smoking in bars and card clubs. We pass a bar on the seedy side of town and find twenty or so good ol' boys — big boys with tatts, broken teeth and beer guts — all standing in the street smoking in the rain while inside the bar is empty.

Meanwhile the rats are having a ball. We see them, too, down by the Golden Gate bridge. It's due to a new ordinance. The Department of Environment has banned the use of toxic chemicals on public property. Rodenticides are out. Rats are in. The Department of Public Health officials estimate there is now one rat per person in San Francisco.

What should be done? I think it's obvious. Nothing. With all those smokers puffing away in public places sooner or later the rats will die of passive smoking!

But if you're going to San Francisco be sure to wear a mousetrap in your hair. And a gas mask. And no one will even notice!

Meanwhile we board yet another plane. This time for the long five-hour haul to New York.

IF I CAN MAKE IT (Across the Road) There, I Can Make it Anywhere — New York, New York

I knew I had to be careful in New York. I'd heard the stories. People aren't just robbed in New York, they lose every item of clothing down to their underpants. And, frankly, I didn't think my underpants were up to it. 'Being miserable and treating other people like dirt is every New Yorker's right.' Who said that? The Mayor of New York, in *Ghost Busters II*. But who am I to argue?

Needless to say, I arrive in New York expecting to find a mugger on every corner or, at the very least, to be trampled in between by a stampede of depressed Woody Allens.

The first night, I think I am dead. There is an art to eating out in New York. If you go to a restaurant where no one is waiting, then even the gallon of ketchup on the table will not prevent the food tasting like a bowl full of sundried newspapers topped with melted cheese. If, on the other hand, you go to a popular restaurant, the food is good — possibly in a three-tonne of barbecue ribs sort of way — but you have to wait for a table. One hour. Maybe two.

On the first night we go to Virgil's and squeeze in elbow-to-elbow with the locals at the bar to wait for our table. I'll tell you something about Virgil's. It has a beer menu. They claim to have 104 different beers in stock at Virgil's. You can buy a Blackened Voodoo Lager from New Orleans, Ed's Cave Creek Chilli Beer from Arizona, MacAndrews Scotch Ale from Edinburgh, a Pinkus UR-Weizen (an organic beer) from Germany, or Pete's Wicked Bohemian Pilsner from Minnesota.

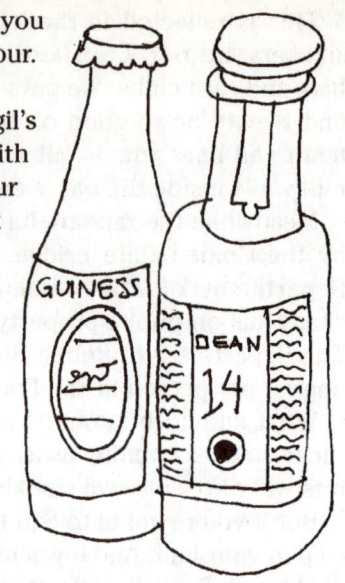

Being a little nostalgic I look for an Aussie beer on the menu. There are none under pale ales, golden, amber or dark lagers. Finally, I find one Aussie beer. Foster's Lager listed under 'Pilseners'. Our lager — a pilsener? And sold by the oilcan. That's what it is called. It is a very big can: 25.4 fl ozs. That's more than a pint, almost a litre. But it passes muster on the description. Malty with a brisk, smooth palate. I am tempted. It sure sounds a lot more appealing than chilli beer.

As we stand crammed like well-dressed sardines in the bar, I make a classic *faux pas*. Watching the telly I take a sip from my neighbour's drink by mistake. I am ready to drop to my knees and plead for my life. 'It's okay, really,' he insists. 'Don't worry.' And so it went. People in New York were truly helpful. Friendly even. At one stage on the subway we have a committee going to try and work out which station we need for the World Trade Centre. I felt like saying, 'Hold on a minute. This is wrong. At this point you're meant to spit in my face.' Instead, of course, I simply acknowledged all this friendliness with genuine, wide-eyed amazement.

Everyone I meet in New York is exceedingly outgoing and helpful. And they all want to come to Australia, so I invite them. The whole fifteen million. Sorry. It is going to be a bit of a tight squeeze!

But there are certain things you should never do in New York. Firstly, never have a heart attack. The traffic is shocking. Echoing through those canyons of skyscrapers, the noise of New York is all honking horns and emergency sirens because the traffic hardly moves. I watch ambulances going nowhere with a lot of noise. If you have a heart attack in New York, take the subway. If a New York motorist sees a slither of open road in front of them, they get so excited, they just don't see any intervening pedestrians. They don't slow down. They don't deviate from their set path. They go for it. So if you are a pedestrian in New York, you don't wait to see the glint of excitement in the motorist's eyes. You run for your life.

If you drive in New York, obey the parking signs. Apart from 'No Standing' the parking signs include 'Do not even think about parking here.' And the traffic cops in New York mean business. You know this because they drive tow trucks.

If you wander into a shop on 5th Avenue, don't look at the price tags or you could have a heart attack. A standard evening dress could be around $A10 000. A woman's suit would be a steal at $A3000. But add a Dolly Parton wig and a strong wind gust, and bingo, you're Ivana Trump. Just around the corner, however, you can buy a denim shirt for $A7. Needless to say, I'm sticking with the Dolly Parton cowgirl look.

If you do go shopping in New York, leave your ghetto-blaster behind. 'No Food. No Drink. No Radio.' I know you will be tempted to rock on down 7th Street past Times Square to bop and shop 'til you drop but you'll have to resist the urge.

Another thing, when in New York don't go to a Broadway show. Around thirty-five Broadway shows run at any one time but twenty-five million people visit New York annually. When you line up in the rain for tickets you will find about seventeen million of them are in the queue ahead of you. We see *Cats*. But it is so exhausting getting tickets when the show finally starts all I feel like saying is, 'Someone stop that bloody cat whining. I'm trying to get some sleep here.'

Don't go up the Empire State Building on a windy day. I did. It was a shock. At one point, there was such an updraught, I thought my knickers had been blown off. And I was standing in the area deemed safe for sightseeing. Another section of the viewing platform was roped off. I leaned around the corner of that section and nearly had my eyebrows blown off. I tell you girls, if you go up the Empire State Building on a windy day, hold on to your eyebrows.

Don't go up the World Trade Centre in fog. What happens is this. You pay $A18, travel at ear-popping speed up 106 floors, and all you see is fog. You could have seen just as much fog for nothing by standing on the ground and looking up.

Finally, if you are arrested in New York, don't worry. There are ads for attorneys everywhere along the lines of: 'For homicide, narcotics, theft, all crimes ring 1-800-GRABTHEMONEYnRUN. Credit cards accepted.' They'll accept credit only if you've robbed the bank first. That's New York.

LIBERTY! She's My Kinda Gal!

We take a ferry trip to the Statue of Liberty. I've seen her so often. She's so familiar. I feel as if she's really my big sister going off to a fancy dress party.

All copper, she's a work of blue-green verdigris art. You'd probably cure arthritis just standing inside her. Yet she stands aloof, a dignified symbol of freedom.

I'm in the museum under her podium trying to get a mental grip on her size. There is a reproduction of her big toe. It's huge. Her torch. Her face. She's a big girl. You can walk inside her head. But every time I line her up in the camera lens she looks like a little souvenir trophy. I can't capture her magnificence.

Look mummy! The lady's got dandruff.

No darling! She's having trouble with the pigeons.

I read about her history. And who should crop up as one of her benefactors? Gustave Eiffel, the French engineer. What's he doing here? It turns out he designed her inner supports so she doesn't blow over in a high wind. Without Gustave, instead of the Statue of Liberty, New Yorkers may well have ended up with the Hunchback of Liberty.

Thanks to Eiffel, she stands tall. A fine tribute to French engineering.

WASHINGTON Centre of The Free World

We board an Amtrak train at Penn Station, New York, and settle in for the three-hour trip that will whisk us down the east coast of America through five states: New York, New Jersey, Pennsylvania (in the distance we glimpse the brilliant facets of the blue crystal towers of Philadelphia city), Maryland, and Washington DC.

Arriving in Washington is an experience, at first, like being trapped in front of a very large television set broadcasting news bulletins from America. You see the classic White House shot, the standard view of the Capitol Hill dome, the regal statue of a seated Lincoln at the Lincoln memorial, the Iwo Jima statue of marines struggling to erect the US flag, the eternal flame at the JFK grave in Arlington Cemetery, even the cliched overhead shot of military helicopters on the move. They fly over from time to time. And you see the American flag everywhere, folding and unfolding in the breeze. These are the images wheeled out time and again to accompany crucial TV news footage.

Yet beyond a mere television cliché, Washington has not only managed to capture fleeting moments of American history in bronze, stone and marble, it *is* history. It is Lincoln's death and Martin Luther King's 'I have a dream' speech and Kennedy's funeral and Watergate. It is the heart, soul and hope of America housed in buildings and shrines of spectacular dignity.

The heart of America can be seen exposed at the Vietnam War memorial. Here the names of the dead are chipped simply into black marble, and ordinary Americans gather to find that one name which still carries with it so much pain and inexpressible grief.

The soul of America is captured in the stone walls of the Lincoln memorial. For here, in full, is recorded Lincoln's Gettysburg address. The vision of America: Unity and Equality and Democracy. And once more, ordinary Americans gather to read the words, but many know them already by heart, and mouth them with respect.

And finally, the hope of America is captured in the Constitution and Bill of Rights which are both reverently housed in the National Archives Rotunda. To see these inked proclamations signed with loopy old-style signatures, knowing that they represent the greatest attempt by a governing body to define the rights of its citizens, is very moving. Housed in the same vaulted-ceiling sanctuary — no other name would do it justice — are other relics of American history.

There is, in part, the agreement signed by the two Generals, Ulysses Grant and Robert E. Lee, at the end of the Civil War. The significance of this document still reverberates throughout the union not because the war did end, but because of how it ended. Both parties agreed, after seven years of war, that on the signing of the document there would be no retribution and no celebration. Soldiers from both sides downed guns and went home. It saved the union.

On reading documents of such significance, you cannot help but feel patriotic even if you aren't American. I cried.

But, in keeping with the American way of recording all history, in the same cabinet, along a bit, were the Watergate bugs. They were Chapsticks (for dry lips) with little wires hanging out of them. They must be the Chapsticks that changed the world. Well, almost.

✈ ✈ ✈ ✈ ✈

Vision is a word set in the foundation stones of many American cities and Washington is no exception. The city is laid out in a grid of such precision and logic, it's a wonder they haven't organised square clouds to roll past with regulation gaps. The north–south streets are named with numbers. The east–west streets are named in alphabetical order, while the diagonal streets are named after the states in the union, the entire fifty. Of course, this naming system can provide a little confusion for the unwary as there is a New York Avenue in Washington and a Washington Place in New York (down at the unnumbered end). You wouldn't want to turn up at the wrong address — you'd be a good three-hour train ride out.

I like this naming of streets alphabetically. You can tell someone in Washington to 'go to L' without any use of profanity because you mean, 'Go to L Street between 14th and 15th near Vermont.'

I also find this idea of numbering rather than naming streets worthwhile. Firstly, if you are taking a young child for a walk in Washington, they will soon learn how to count, especially if you tell this child of the modern motoring era that you are heading for 20th Street, and you start walking at 1st Street.

Secondly, if you are a tourist like myself with no sense of direction then this streets-named-by-number concept can take a lot of the confusion out of getting lost — you can get lost in numerical order!

✈ ✈ ✈ ✈ ✈

Wandering around the stately glory of Washington, I am glad that I am neither a student of art or architecture. I can appreciate Washington for the immediate impact of its grand gestures in architecture rather than feel obliged to judge the structures as hotch-potch amalgams of Baroque, Greek revival or French Second Empire style with excesses of marble and gilt, as described in various guidebooks.

Reading these books makes me wonder, 'Where is the rule book that says Doric columns cannot be used outside of Greece?' Or where is it written that only architecture committed to the trends of its time reflects a true sophistication in taste? I feel Washington, the home of the Constitution, lives up to the spirit of the Constitution, in every stone slab and whim of the architecture. It represents to me freedom in grand architectural thinking and reflects that very American attitude, namely, when it comes to people, ideas and attitudes, we'll take the lot. And I revel in every Doric column.

Of course, Freedom herself suffered a little re-engineering on her way to sit in bronze glory on top of the Capital dome. It is all to do with her hat. She's a tall girl at 5.8 metres, and a fairly solid girl too, being bronze. In the original drawings she sported a cap worn by freed Roman slaves and French revolutionaries. This was viewed by some in those pre-civil war days as an incitement for slaves to revolt. So she got a different hat. A plumed Roman-soldier type affair. But I say bring back the cap.

The girl should be given a baseball cap!

✈ ✈ ✈ ✈ ✈

Washington is so magnificent, so historic, so moving, you can't help feeling it should be set to a soundtrack. And it is. You can stand behind the White House and listen to the speakers in the garden play a little music, perhaps the Marines Anthem, followed by a commentary on the garden's history, something about the weddings that have taken place in the White House, and stories about the various pets Presidents have owned including a snake and a bear.

Under the Lincoln Memorial beside the toilets you will find a display and a commentary on various events that have taken place at the memorial. Everywhere; commentaries and music.

But there is an openness about Washington that is unequalled in other cities. The founding fathers of Washington had the vision, again, to stipulate that no building may be built higher than the Captial dome. It is, in consequence, a low-rise city.

There is another form of openness that can be found only in America. The White House is open to the public on a regular basis. We line up with teary-eyed Americans — it is a crisp morning in February and many in the queue have the sniffles — and within three-quarters of an hour we are standing looking out of the South Portico at the gardens. We are gawking from the second floor windows in the round-columned section of the White House with the flag on top seen in every classic shot of the Presidential Residence. I can't believe it. With so little fuss, we are standing on the blue oval carpet in the dead centre of the White House, or to be more accurate, in the middle of that vision of the White House blown up in every alien invasion movie ever made in America.

We are in an oval room in the middle of the White House, but we aren't in the Oval Office. The Oval Office is tucked away in the West Wing. This upsets my vision of the White House. I always imagined the President to be sitting working right in the middle of the White House, not tucked away in a broom closet somewhere else.

But I can say security is taken very seriously in the White House. Very seriously indeed. It is protected by the US Secret Service and members of the US Secret Service uniformed division. I know this because they tell you on the sign out the front. But for a Secret Service they are not that secret. In fact, I'd say, bloody obvious. You see swat-like uniformed agents, armed and dressed completely in black, patrolling the grounds from time to time. And you can fairly easily tell the difference between a gardener and a Secret Service agent. Here's a hint. The gardeners do not walk around armed with laser-aim rakes.

While inside the White House you can play spot the Secret Service agent. But it's not much of a game, they are so obvious: crew-cut hair, grey suit, thin tie, and with a little squiggly thing coming out of one ear. I don't think they employ Secret Service agents to work in the White House. I suspect they go to a casting agency.

Despite the obvious, security is tight. Taking no chances here are fifteen items listed as prohibited inside the White House. There will be:

- No food or beverages
- No photography
- No videotaping
- No animals (except guide dogs)
- No smoking
- No suitcases or duffle bags
- No strollers (checked at gate)
- No backpacks (over-sized)
- No electric stun guns
- No firecrackers or fireworks
- No guns or ammunition
- No knives with blades over 3 inches/8 cm
- No Mace
- No nunchakus
- No balloons

Have I missed something here? No balloons? Have you ever heard anyone yell 'Stand back everybody. I'm holding a balloon,' or 'This is a stick-up. I've got a balloon in my pocket?'

HRH points out that only a card-carrying idiot would walk into the White House carrying something that might go 'Bang' by mistake. Boy, would they be the centre of attention or what? But they don't ban paper bags. You could smuggle a paper bag into the White House, blow it up and end up just as popular.

The security is good, but I don't know if they have covered everything. What about No pitchforks, No bazookas, No armed nuclear warheads?

Nevertheless, if you meet me in the street, I'll demand respect. I got into the White House. And I'll tell you what, they may have banned nunchakus but you should see what I can do with the underwire from a bra cup.

AND I WENT INTO THE WHITE HOUSE ARMED WITH TWO OF THEM!

✈ ✈ ✈ ✈ ✈

Washington is indisputably the Centre of the Free World. I'll tell you why. Everything's free — every monument, every museum — free entry. White House; free. National Gallery of Art; free. National Museum of Natural History; free. National Museum of American History; free. Freer Gallery of Art; couldn't be freer!

> They landed on the moon in an aluminium pie dish with legs.

The National Air and Space Museum is also free to visit. In the foyer of this museum hangs the fabric and wood first-ever manned, powered aeroplane — the Wright Flyer. There is also Lindberg's Spirit of St Louis and the returned Apollo 11 Command Module. This museum holds the history of aviation in one foyer. Aerospace fanatics would crawl the length of Route 66, and pay with their grandmother, to view such awe-inspiring milestones of aviation history. And it's free. They also have the moon module there. Not *the* moon module. It didn't make it back to earth. But a moon module built at the same time for tests that were never conducted. It gave me a lot more respect for Neil Armstrong and

Co. They landed on the moon in an aluminium pie dish with legs. It was thrown together with tin foil and sticky tape. I've seen ironing boards that look more substantial than the moon module. After seeing the moon module, I'm scrubbing going to the moon off my list of things to do in retirement, I tell you. I'm sticking with ironing boards.

You can visit the FBI headquarters. They'll show you their collection of 35 000 guns. An agent will even fire a gun for you. And it's free. There can, unfortunately, be a long wait in summer, but, if you pretend to kidnap the person in front of you in the queue, you will end up in the FBI headquarters much faster with free demonstrations of fingerprint taking, mugshot art and a private tour of an interview room. You might even end up with free accommodation for the night.

I cannot, however, over-emphasise the significance of free entry to the wallet-weary traveller. I had to pay to see the Crown Jewels in the Tower of London. As an Australian, I can still say the Queen is my Queen. We pay. We have payed 'royalties' for many years. I would say we in Australia own, at least, one full quarter of one of the lesser tiaras. Still, we have to pay to see the Crown Jewels.

But, in Washington, America's heritage is on view for free. This can be dangerous for the over-enthusiastic traveller who can easily overdose on exposure to, say, modern art. Try to pace yourself, ration the museums, limit yourself to a couple of Jackson Pollocks and the odd Warhol, don't overdo the sculptures, and limit the number of historical artefacts, and you will survive the free world. But only just.

✈ ✈ ✈ ✈ ✈

I'm not listening to my own advice. I'm overdosing on history in the National Archives Rotunda, Washington, DC. This building is a fabulous cross between the Pantheon and the Vatican.

In awed reverence I view the Declaration of Independence, the Constitution and the Bill of Rights. I can read the date on the Declaration of Independence: July 4, 1776. The pettiness of every-day irritations vanishes as my heart is lifted by the grand vision of good men. I congratulate the nearest American. The guard. He accepts on behalf of 250 million Americans.

Then I turn to view one more document. One nearer the gift-shop. What is it? The Magna Carta.

THE MAGNA CARTA! The foundation stone of English law. The charter written in Latin that established the concept that all men (unfortunately women took a few more centuries to catch up) were equal before the law. Written in 1297, this was no four score and seven years ago our forefathers. This document was signed four score and seven years plus six good centuries ago, give or take.

What the bloody hell was the Magna Carta doing in Washington? It was written nearly five centuries before George Washington was in short pants. I would have been just as flabbergasted if the Gettysburg Address had turned up in a museum at Reading, UK. But there it is. The Magna Carta is in Washington. Apparently, it was written out more that once and this version was bought in 1984 by businessman Ross Perot and loaned to the Archive centre. But they haven't got the Crown Jewels, yet.

VOTE 1 Barbie For President

One of the greatest contrasts between American and Australian culture, which screams out at me everywhere I go, is the immense enthusiasm and respect Americans show for their country, their flag and their military history.

This respect is reflected in the hushed reverence that cloaks the interior of the Lincoln Memorial. Americans are moved to be there. Looking up at the mammoth six-metre statue of the seated Lincoln, I couldn't help but think about how we revere our Prime Ministers in Australia. We don't. Of course, no Australian Prime Minister has been assassinated in the line of duty, so that dimension in drama is absent from the history books.

The only memorial I can think of is the Harold Holt Swimming Pool in Melbourne. We have managed, in Australia, to dedicate a swimming pool to the Prime Minister who drowned in office. If we've gone that far, I don't know why we don't put a statue of him at the bottom of the pool.

Of course, all of this presidential awe and respect can manifest itself in strange ways. There's Mt Rushmore. This place is amazing to Australians. We are usually so darn glad to get rid of our

Prime Ministers there is no way we would carve their heads in a mountainside unless we could go there, perhaps, and throw tomatoes at it. My favourite presidential salute is the George Washington Barbie Doll. Every year for some years now Mattel have made a commemorative Barbie doll for Presidents' Day turning Barbie (brainless, busty, bottle-blond Barbie) into the only female who has been President of America. George Washington Barbie is gorgeous in 'her' little knickerbocker pants and knee-high stockings. Again, to an Australian, this is beyond belief. We would never have a Barbie doll named after one of our parliamentary founding fathers. Firstly, because we couldn't remember their names. And secondly, because most of our Prime Ministers have been far too short to be a Barbie doll, even in high heels.

This idea of a Presidential Barbie doll has great appeal for me. I can't wait until they bring out an Abraham Lincoln Barbie. It's a girl thing. I would just love to see Barbie with a beard!

While on the subject of dolls I am also taken by the GI Joe Classic Collection. There is a historical Commander's edition which includes General Dwight D. Eisenhower, boxed with helmet, little US Army flag and little American flag, and General George S. Patton, complete with little riding crop, pearl-handled pistol and three-star helmet. I couldn't help but marvel at the grasp Americans have of their own history. Any attempt to do something like this in Australia would have kids saying 'General who?'

To see pride in the American flag in Washington is not surprising. It is, after all, the seat of government. Even so, to walk out of the grand cavernous interior of the old Union Station and see four flag poles topped with gold eagles all flying the stars and stripes, the whole pageant lit by golden rays from the setting sun, is like being hit with a jolt from an emotional stun gun.

I was in New York on Presidents' Day and I swear there were more flags on 5th Avenue than exist in Australia. They were lined up across shopfronts, and adorning churches. As for the Fourth of July, it's a wonder pigeons don't drop out of the sky mesmerised by all of those moving stars and stripes.

Whereas we in Australia do not fuss over our flag. We are trying to work up some enthusiasm for Australia Day, if we could remember when it was. It's in the summer break, I believe. At present, the only way many Australians get to see their flag on Australia Day is if someone has it printed on a beach towel at the beach.

DAMNED LIES AND STATISTICS
or More About Sex and Americans

I cannot visit America without commenting on the very curious topic of sex and Americans. Are Americans obsessed by sex and sexual harassment issues? Maybe. I can tell you one thing for sure. Americans are obsessed with statistics about sex. And the statistics tell an interesting story.

Try this one. A typical adult American is more likely on a given day to have prayed than had sex. The nation that gave us films like *Basic Instinct* and *When Harry Met Sally* prays more than it tumbles in the hay. They should be making films like 'Basic Instinct to Pray' and 'When Harry Met St Cecilia'. America is not the freewheeling society Australians sometimes imagine. Only ten out of fifty states in America have anti-discrimination laws protecting gays.

In America, religion is taken very seriously indeed. This is the country where you can buy a board game called 'Bibleopoly'. You do not go to gaol in this game. You 'Go to Meditate'. I don't know what you get when you 'pass go'. I suppose you just stop and pass around the plate.

A book that has spent some time on the *New York Times* best-sellers list is *Talking to Heaven* by self-proclaimed psychic James Van Praagh. It's not how I picture heaven but as soon as I read the title, I realise, of course, these days St Peter would be standing at the pearly gates with a mobile phone. I read *USA Today* which reports on surveys that show people who attend church regularly live longer, enjoy better mental health, and are less likely to suffer from cancer. Obviously, praying is good for your health.

What about sex? Well, it's good for your health too.

According to an article in the *New Yorker* when the classic reference for psychiatrists, *DSM-I*, came out in 1952 homosexuality and nymphomania were listed as mental disorders. Not now. By 1980, many mental disorders listed in the *DSM-III* are related to not getting enough sex such as anorgasmia. So sex is good for your health. But how do you get it?

First, according to the statistics, it helps if you are male. Or, maybe American men are just more enthusiastic about filling in forms relating to sexual statistics. Whatever the case, here are the results. American researchers hired attractive assistants to approach students on various college campuses and proposition them out-of-the-blue. What proportion said 'yes'? Zero per cent of women; and seventy-five per cent of men (with many of the remaining twenty-five per cent asking for a raincheck).

A University of Chicago survey reported that Americans who indulge in more sex than the average include jazz enthusiasts (is this more damning evidence against Bill Clinton, who plays the saxophone?); the less educated (as the level of education increases Americans are less active sexually, so that we can only conclude that university professors have risen to the ranks of the educationally neutered); those who are in a lower income group; people who are married, who smoke and/or drink more than average, or who watch lots of TV. You may not have realised this, but the all-American stud is actually Homer Simpson.

American women who enjoy more sex than average own guns. But this is unnecessary. They don't have to proposition a man at gunpoint to have sex. The surveys all show he'll say 'yes' anyway.

And those Americans who enjoy more sex are not regular churchgoers.

I can only conclude from all of these surveys that there are two groups of Americans. One lot goes to church regularly to pray, and they live longer. The other lot overdo the drinking, smoking and TV-watching, and they die younger, but they all go out with a 'bang', presumably.

Where does sexual harassment fit into this picture? Well, it's a complicated issue but I learned something about sexual harrassment American-style while touring the states. A woman from Des Moines, Iowa, brought a case against her employer, the United Parcel Service, and won. The greatest physical abuse she suffered was having her breast poked by a subordinate's finger. She was awarded $US80.7 million ($A118 million). Appeals are pending. But forget religion. Forget the moral issues. Obviously, in America, sexual harassment is big business.

So there it is. There are two groups of Americans. Those who pray and live longer. And those who smoke, drink, have sex and die young. But is this the whole story? No. There is still the issue of mental health. Sex is good for your mental health. The group who go to church regularly, but do not smoke, drink or have sex overly much, enjoy good mental health. How can this be? The answer is obvious. They must be praying for sex!

LOST IN THE KNICKERS OF TIME

Before I leave America, I must come clean on the knickers issue and tell you the tale of my knickers and their destiny as mapped out by the fates in New York.

On the plane travelling into New York, a startlingly reckless idea inserts itself into my brain like an alien lava form. It grows and grows. This pulsating idea spawns a fiendishly devious plot which will add colour and confusion to my New York experience.

The idea is simple; that I should call the book I am planning to write, 'I left my heart in ... in ... in Chinkapook.' 'Oh yes,' I say to myself, 'and I'll probably leave my knickers in New York.' That's when the 300-watt light bulb lights up above my head. 'Now there's a title,' I say to myself, *I Left My Heart in Chinkapook and My Knickers in New York.*'

With the dawning of this title comes a grave responsibility. I feel duty-bound to live up to the claim to jettison, with elegance and flair, a pair of knickers in New York. And I have to tell you, trying to abandon a pair of knickers in New York is not as easy as you first think.

I buy a G-string. Black with red lace. I feel a G-string is required for this subversive operation as it is alluring. Sexy. And I have my pride. Chucking a pair of full brief cottontails off the top of the Empire State Building seems somehow more like the first sign of senility than an act of wild abandon.

The second reason for buying a G-string is personal. Whenever I get around to buying new knickers, my old knickers suddenly look, in comparison, as if they must have spent the last two years of life as warning rags dangling from sewerage pipes on a plumber's van. In other words, if I bought a pair of half decent, vaguely wearable knickers, I wouldn't be able to part with them. It is decided. A G-string will have to be sacrificed for the cause — to end its life on the streets of New York.

Unfortunately, this brilliant plot is a logistical nightmare. Carrying a G-string around in my handbag leads to multiple complications. While otherwise occupied taking money, keys, passport or pen out of the handbag, I manage to execute a gaggle of absurdities.

Trying to pay a restaurant bill, I nearly flick a waiter in the eye with the G-string. I manage to catapult a tampon across a subway cashier's booth. I remove my wallet from the handbag and try to nonchalantly pay a cab fare with the G-string sticking out either end of the wallet like a hot dog. And, on yet another occasion, I have to open my hotel room with the G-string entwined in the key ring and hanging limply down the door.

Needless to say, I was working up an almost obsessive level of enthusiasm for getting rid of the G-string. Unfortunately, the ideal ceremonial moment for the chucking of the G-string keeps evading me.

I think I might drop it over the side of the Ellis Island Ferry into the Hudson River. I soon realise, however, that the trip to Ellis Island is a highly emotional journey for those millions of Americans who can trace their family history back through the immigrant centre to a plethora of impoverished homelands. I couldn't stand on the deck twirling a G-string. It is too irreverent.

Trying to pay a restaurant bill, I nearly flick a waiter in the eye with my G-string.

I decide to chuck the G-string off the Statue of Liberty. It would be a symbolic gesture associating freedom and liberty with the feminist gesture of dumping ridiculously uncomfortable lingerie. But Liberty's head is closed for the day. We only make it to her bustline. I have to hold on to my knickers for one more day.

The Empire State Building is useless. The open viewing area on the ninety-sixth floor is completely caged off, and it is blowing a gale. Not only would I have to spend time forcing my knickers through a little cage hole, I was worried that the G-string might land on the head of an innocent pedestrian ninety-six floors below. It might cause immeasurable psychological harm. It would, if the guy on the street thought it had started raining knickers and G-strings in New York.

Times Square is no help. There are too many buskers. I am very concerned that if I start waving a G-string in the air in Times Square, people might start applauding and throwing money at me.

I thought the Brooklyn Bridge might be the go. But the walkway is suspended over three billion lanes of traffic. Even if I threw my knickers with all my might, they would never make it to the river. They'd probably land on the windscreen wipers of a truck and cause a diabolical pile up on one of Manhattan's major arteries.

The World Trade Centre is hopeless. The outdoor walkway is closed. All I could do was stand on the 106th floor and wipe my knickers across the glass.

Towards the end of our stay in New York, I gave up the idea of grand gestures. I would simply dump the G-string in a trash can at the airport. Then I would have done my duty for book and country and no one would be the wiser. But, alas, a subliminal desire had been buried deep in my psyche. I could not escape my subconscious desire to experience the unbearable lightness of being knickerless in New York.

On the last day in New York, I jump out of bed and tell my family that I'm going shopping. I'd concentrated my conscious thoughts so intensely on losing my knickers in New York, I had forgotten about needing other clothes. And the winter sales are on. Two for one at Bloomingdales. Resistance is futile.

I have two hours, four credit cards, and no sense of direction. I bolt out of the hotel door with HRH (His Royal Huffiness) inhaling with such an intensity of indignation, I fear he might swallow his own lips. 'I'll have the taxi waiting,' he snorts to a closing door.

I run up 44th Street, charge down 5th Avenue, gallop along 50th Street, and sprint up 7th Avenue. I have this vague feeling that I am running around in circles. But it doesn't matter. There are sales to the right of me. Bargains to the left of me. Mark-downs in front of me. I fling myself into the jaws of discount, into the mouth of hope. I spy a $600 price tag marked down to $300: a lined suit. Very nice. And a shirt. And a skirt. And some slacks.

I storm the fitting rooms laden with armfuls of hope and glory. Half-dressed and half getting undressed, I hop around the narrow confines of the fitting room on one foot trying to get a foot in or out of a pair of pants while trying on six other outfits at the same time.

When I try on a *faux* fur coat with the hanger still in it (it made me look like an elk across the shoulders), I think I should slow down. But I can't. No time. I rush out into the shop half-dressed, grab another armful of bargains and bolt back into the fitting room dropping mini-skirts and lace shirts like autumn leaves along my path. This is a shopping frenzy. Two pairs of jeans, three skivvies, a jumper, and a business suit. The jeans were $29. Even if the Aussie dollar decided to have a heart attack and collapse while we were away, the jeans are still a bargain.

And I salute the sizing policies of American jeans manufacturers. I suspect it's written into the Constitution. It's the democratic right of every girl in America to have a bottom. And American jean manufacturers, bless them all, recognise this right.

Finally, ten New York blocks away from our hotel, the Algonquin on 44th, with five minutes to spare and two shirts to buy, I rip off my old crutch-cruncher denims, and, still dancing around on one foot, scramble into my new bargain BLF (Bum Liberation Front) jeans. I run my credit card through its last hoorah, grab a confusion of carry bags and bolt. Even as I stride down 7th, I marvel at the absolute jean comfort. I could have written an Ode to Bottom Joy. But there is no time.

I round the corner at 44th. The taxi is waiting. It is blowing its horn. HRH is waiting and he is blowing a mental gasket. I throw myself and packages into the back seat of the yellow cab. On the way to the railway station and a new adventure, I suddenly realise why these jeans give me a new and fascinating sensation of total freedom. No knickers. I'd managed to lose them in a fitting room frenzy. Somewhere along 44th, down 7th Avenue, around 50th or somewhere in between, in the shadowy interior of a department store fitting room lies one pair of Aussie Target undies, crumpled and forlorn. Abandoned in New York.

MISSING YOU ALREADY, AMERICA

There were times in America when I would stand in a street looking at signs for Safeway, K-Mart, McDonald's, Pizza Hut and Coca Cola, and think, 'Hell. I haven't left home.'

At other times I would stand there thinking, 'I've landed on a planet entirely peopled by "Melrose Place" clones and stage-managed by Steven Spielberg.' I find America is often so far-out. One visit to Times Square in New York proved to embody such an experience.

There in the heart of New York, at the epicentre of grand confusion where 42nd Street, 7th Avenue and Broadway intersect, is Times Square. It is a cacophony of street theatre lit at night by a hysteria of neon signs. A giant video screen broadcasts news footage with a word summary constantly rolling beneath. When we are there, a giant, internally lit, three-dimensional Cup-o-Noodle cup, leans impossibly out from one building into Times Square with steam pouring out the top. NYPD's finest are well represented and blow their whistles to an almost rhythmic beat. And pedestrians scurry in every direction in a permanent pantomime of haste.

It is our first day in New York and we see a spaceship landing on the very small triangular traffic island in the middle of the bedlam of Times Square. Roads are blocked. Car horns toot. And out of the spaceship step four silver-suited astronauts. But there are cameras and action. They are filming an ad for a new ride at Sea World!

This is America. From the humdrum to the spectacular, America is, for the Aussie tourist, a truly mind-bending experience. As I pack my bags for home, colourful images of America flash constantly inside my brain as if someone has installed the giant video screen from Times Square in my head.

Even as I rest my bags at the airline check-in counter in Washington, I feel a weight of sadness that we are leaving such a spectactularly bizarre culture for the familiar comfort of home.

EPILOGUE

Arriving at this point in the book has the same numbness about it as that feeling you get when the plane hits the tarmac on the home trip. The tour is over. Finished, for now.

So I have to ask, 'Does travel solve life's problems?' Of course, not. Life's problems are sitting around waiting for you at home in a pile in the letterbox. Not only that, the sewerage has probably blocked, the car battery is flat, there's no food in the house, and that stack of mail includes reminders for all the fun things you have postponed but have to face sometime — like the visit to the dentist and the optician and, for us girls, add that riot of excitement, that fun trip to the gynaecologist, and the accountant and so on and on. Life cannot be ignored indefinitely.

But what travel offers the traveller is a sort of 'spring-cleaning of the soul', which can bring new vigour into drab corners of your life. Especially in those middle years.

For many of us, what happens as we drag our souls through the decades is that we whisk them through the high-spirited twenties, settle them down for the family-oriented thirties to arrive eventually at the threshold of mid-life with a soul squeezed — possibly trapped — within the confines of multiple responsibilities. The children. The mortgage. Your parents' failing health. Your job. The house guttering. The dog. A local civic group, perhaps. Your own fitness. The garden. Tax forms. The car. Professional development. Recycling. Your not-quite-what-it-should-be-superannuation funds. The renovations. And more.

Even as I write this list I can feel my soul shrinking under the pressure of it all. Responsibility is not necessarily soul destroying, however. There is another factor which arrives by stealth with life's many responsibilities. Familiarity. As we move about life's chores, responsibility wears pathways of bland familiarity into our brains. In a bland landscape any responsibilities loom large and out of proportion. But travel can change that perspective.

Travel has a magical dimension, which sets life's many worries against a much grander backdrop. On a world scale your own worries often shrink into more manageable lots. You can hardly worry about your own guttering when you are looking at the duomo in Florence. You worry a little less about your own health when you see the street beggars of Paris, San Francisco, Hong Kong, anywhere.

And this is what travel can achieve. A bit more room for your soul to breath. Freedom. I'll see you on the next flight.